Enid Mills 8866 9518
bought Oxford Feb. '07

CW00385442

BETWEEN THE WIND AND THE WATER

This book is for Rosa, Guille, Maddie and Harry,
who have had a lot of fun among the stones.
I hope you will continue to enjoy them for years to come.

Between the Wind and the Water

World Heritage Orkney

Caroline Wickham-Jones

WINDgather
PRESS

Between the Wind and the Water: World Heritage Orkney

Text Copyright © Caroline Wickham-Jones 2006

Illustrations Copyright © Orkney Museums and Heritage
unless otherwise indicated.

Windgather Press Ltd acknowledges the support of Orkney Museums and
Heritage in making the publication of this book possible.

All rights reserved. No part of this publication may be reproduced, stored
in a retrieval system, or transmitted in any form or by any means (whether
electronic, mechanical, photocopying or recording) or otherwise without
the written permission of both the publisher and the copyright holder.

Published by: Windgather Press Ltd, 29 Bishop Road, Bollington,
Macclesfield, Cheshire SK10 5NX

Distributed by: Central Books Ltd, 99 Wallis Road, London E9 5LN

British Library Cataloguing-in-Publication Data
A catalogue record for this book is available from the British Library

ISBN 10: 1-905119-06-2
ISBN 13: 978-1-905119-06-6

Designed, typeset and originated by Carnegie Publishing Ltd,
Chatsworth Road, Lancaster

Printed and bound by CPI Bath

Contents

List of Illustrations

Figures

Picture Credits

Gunnie Moberg: front cover.

Raymond Parks: 3, 4, 5, 6, 9, 10, 22, 23, 28, 31, 32, 39, 40, 41, 43, 44, 65, 66, 67, 69, 70, 71.

Sigurd Towrie: 1, 11, 15, 36, 38, 48, 51, 53, 55, 57, 59, 63, 68, 89.

Charles Tait: back cover, 21, 34, 35, 37.

The Orkney Library and Archive Photographic Library: 2, 12, 42a, 74, 75, 76, 77, 78, 79, 80, 81.

Orkney Museums and Heritage: Maps 1–5, 46, 50, 54, 62, 64.

Orkney Archaeological Trust: 14, 58, 60, 61, 83, 84, 85.

Alexandra Shepherd: 29, 30.

Trustees of the National Museums of Scotland: 18, 19, 24, 27.

University of Dundee Archive Services: 86.

Historic Scotland: 24, 26.

Imperial War Museum: 72.

J. N. Graham Ritchie: 82.

John Leith: 33, 42b, 88.

Author: 7, 13, 16, 17, 20, 25, 45, 47, 49, 52, 56, 87.

Acknowledgements

....

Many people know more about Orkney archaeology than I do. I've drawn heavily on published work, websites, and people's generosity. In addition to those named below, there is a thriving body of archaeologists who live and work in Orkney and it will be clear as you read through the book that it is impossible to piece together the story of the World Heritage Sites in Orkney without making use of other people's work: they are all to be thanked. As ever any faults in interpretation or omission are mine!

In particular I would like to thank Sigurd Towrie who put up with a stream of email questions, was happy to discuss various theories, and has provided some brilliant photos. Anne Brundle has helped considerably with archaeological information, and both Tom Muir and Sigurd were very kind regarding my attempt at rewriting the 'story of the stones'. Sarah Jane Gibbon kindly assisted with much of the information for chapter 9, no mean feat while she was putting together her own research on this period for her thesis!

Steve Callaghan kindly agreed to Orkney Museums and Heritage support for the book in terms of assistance with illustration and the production of the maps.

At a more personal level, I did ask several friends to read through various chapters. Their forbearance while looking for my faults has been wonderful and their comments, as ever, were a great help to me. Sarah Jane Gibbon, Jill Harden and Kate Towsey have all encouraged me to go on writing and contributed considerably to the readability of the text and the accuracy of its contents.

The illustrations owe much to many people who generously made their work available. I should like to acknowledge the remarkable work of Raymond Parks whose illustrations were available through Orkney Museums and Heritage. Bobby Leslie, Sarah Jane Gibbon and David Mackie at Orkney Library and Archive all helped with picture research and reproduction there. Anne Brundle and Tom Muir kindly helped with the pictures of artefacts from the Orkney Museum. Kenny Swinney of Orkney Islands Council produced the magnificent maps and diagrams. Orkney Archaeological Trust, through the offices of Nick Card, kindly provided illustrations relating to their work. Lekky Shepherd has been studying the Neolithic art and redrew her illustrations of pot decoration and the art at Skara Brae for me. Both Sigurd Towrie and Charles Tait have generously contributed photographs from their specialised picture collections. John Leith took great trouble to get

Acknowledgements the right aerial photograph to duplicate Low's eighteenth century drawing. The late Graham Ritchie supplied illustrations of his excavation work at the Stones of Stenness.

Various institutions have contributed, especially in the form of copyright permissions: the National Museum of Scotland; Orkney Islands Council; Orkney Library and Archive; Orkney Museums and Heritage; Imperial War Museum; Historic Scotland; Dundee University Archive. I am very grateful to them all.

It is impossible to write without acknowledging a huge debt to Daphne Lorimer, a good friend who provided such inspiration. Her sad death while I was writing this volume has left a big gap in Orkney archaeology.

FIGURE I.
View of the Ring of Brodgar, looking towards the bridge of Brodgar where the loch of Stenness meets Harray Loch.

SIGURD TOWRIE

The Story

....

The Giants of Brodgar

Many, many, years ago, a group of giants made their way across the centre of Orkney, with the Loch of Stenness on their left and the Loch of Harray on their right. They picked their way carefully across the water where the two lochs meet and followed the narrow neck of land up to the higher ground where it opens out. This was a good place for a dance.

One of their number took out his fiddle and stood to one side, another stopped by the lochs for fear of intruders, and they danced! It was a good reel – an Orkney reel. Faster and faster it went until they joined hands and danced in a circle. Round and round they went. High above them Orion the hunter smiled out of the starry night-time sky. All thoughts of daylight left their heads and they gave themselves up to the tunes.

So taken were the giants by their revels that they did not notice as the sky began to lighten and the stars one by one disappeared. With a gentle touch the first rays of the sun spread out across the watery landscape. With a sudden jolt the giants' dance was stopped. As the sun passed over each one they were turned to stone.

They are there to this day, most of them. You can visit them in their frozen dance. Sadly they stare out in an attempt to leave. Sometimes, as you depart, if you turn back quietly, you can almost make out the strains of movement through the low-lying mists as they try to escape their imprisonment. Sometimes you can almost hear the notes of the fiddler as he stands alone on a low mound at the Comet Stone. And at Hogmanay the giant at the Watch Stone, by the bridge of Brodgar, breaks his fast on the stroke of midnight to drink from the loch.

But you will never quite see him.

The Visit

....

Barry, 1805

The Mainland, towards the west, is intersected from south to north, to the distance of nearly five miles, by the loch of Stennis, which, near the middle is almost divided into two, by the plains on each side stretching out, and nearly meeting with each other. These plains are pleasantly situated in the bosom of the loch, and in the centre of an immense amphitheatre, in the area of which are the parishes of Stennis, Harra, and Birsa. Its limits are the hills of Orphir, Rendal, and Sandwick, and the majestic hills of Hoy, which, toward the south, lye at a much greater distance, and bound the prospect. That on the west side of the loch contains a circle sixty fathoms in diameter, formed by a ditch on the outside, twenty feet broad and twelve deep; and on the inside, by a range of standing stones, twelve or fourteen feet high, and four broad; several of them are fallen down, of others fragments remain, and of some only the holes in which they stood. The earth that has been taken from the ditch has been carried away, and very probably been made use of to form four tumuli, or barrows, of considerable magnitude, which are ranked in pairs at the east and west side of this remarkable monument of antiquity.

The plain on the east border of the loch exhibits a semicircle, sixteen

FIGURE 2.
A nineteenth-century view of the Ring of Brodgar (from Fergusson 1898, *A visit to Orcadia*).

COURTESY OF THE ORKNEY LIBRARY AND ARCHIVE PHOTOGRAPHIC LIBRARY

fathoms in diameter, formed not, like the circle, with a ditch, but by a mound of earth, and with stones in the inside, like the former in shape, though of much larger dimensions. Near the circle, there are standing stones that seem to be placed in no regular order that we can now discern; and as near the semi-circle are others of the same description. In one of the latter is a round hole, not in the middle, but towards one of the edges, much worn, as if by the friction of a rope or chain, by which some animal had been bound. Toward the centre of the semicircle, too, is a very large broad stone now lying on the ground; but whether it stood formerly like those around it, or has been raised and supported on pillars to serve a particular purpose, we shall not take upon us to determine.

G. Barry (1805) *History of the Orkney Islands*, 209–10.

MAP 1.
The location of Orkney, off the north coast of Scotland.
KENNY SWINNEY

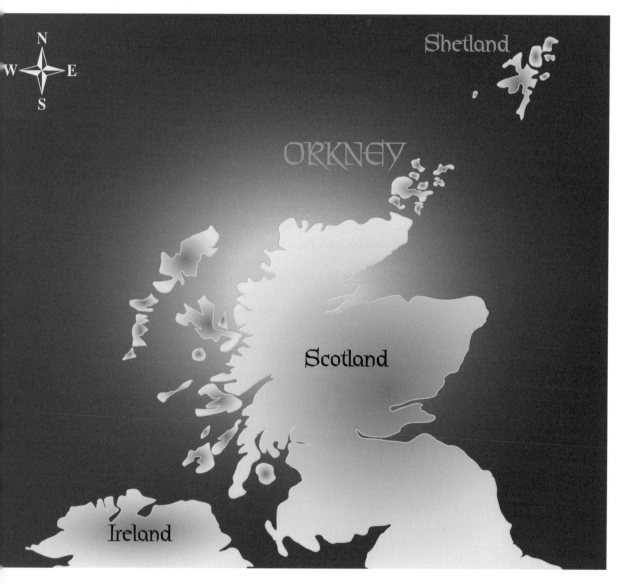

CHAPTER ONE

Orkney and its World Heritage

Setting the scene

In December 1999 a group of sites known as *The Heart of Neolithic Orkney* was inscribed on the World Heritage list. This formal language means that these sites – Skara Brae; The Ring of Brodgar; the Stones of Stenness and adjacent stones; and Maeshowe – are recognized as among the most outstanding ancient monuments in the world. The Convention concerning the protection of the World Cultural and Natural Heritage was adopted by UNESCO in 1972 and is administered by the International Council on Monuments and Sites (ICOMOS), which has branches in many countries (http://www.icomos.org/ICOMOS_Main_Page.html).

World Heritage sites occur in most countries. More are added to the list every year. Sites can be specific locations, or they may be wider areas, and they are recognized on the grounds of cultural or natural heritage, or a combination of the two. It is not the intention of this volume to look in detail at the processes by which sites are put forward, nor at World Heritage sites on a global basis. World Heritage is discussed briefly in Chapter Twelve, and plenty of other works look at it in more detail (see the Notes to the Chapters).

The sites of Neolithic Orkney are some 5,000 years old, and were built by the Stone Age farmers of the islands. This book will look at them and at what

FIGURE 3.
The Ring of Brodgar today.
RAYMOND PARKS

makes them so special. It is intended to provide a guide to the ways in which the sites functioned, the world in which they were built, how they came to be a focus through the ages, and what they mean today.

Orkney

Orkney comprises a group of islands that lie about seven miles from the north coast of Scotland (Map 1). There are approximately 70 islands, ranging from the largest, Mainland, some 20 miles by 15 miles, to small rocky skerries and grassy holms. In the early twenty-first century about 20 of these islands are inhabited by a scattered population of some 20,000 people. It is possible that the population of Neolithic Orkney was about the same.

Geology

In general Orkney is low-lying. It is mostly made up of ancient sandstones, formed in a warm shallow sea about 380 million years ago, when this area lay closer to the tropics.[1] One result of this is that fossils abound across the islands. Fossil fish and the remains of vegetation are to be found in many quarry sites, though it is no longer possible to remove them at will; due to the popularity of fossil hunting, many of the geological sites were disappearing and so they are now protected by law (Figure 4).

Another aspect of the Orkney sandstones is that building materials are plentiful across the islands. Orkney sandstone has clear bedding planes and naturally splits into rectangular slabs with which it is easy to work. This has had a marked effect on the historic landscape. It was not difficult to extract stone and small quarry pits are plentiful, while stone built dwellings are to be seen everywhere. In prehistory the stone was just as useful: the inhabitants of Neolithic Orkney not only built their houses of stone, they used stone for internal partitions and for furniture as well. This has not led to 'Flintstones'-inspired remains; rather, it has provided a wealth of information on the sophistication and ingenuity of the past that is just not evident elsewhere in Scotland, where people built with less durable materials. Stone was also used to build great monuments: the circles of standing stones and the domed tombs for the dead that completed the sphere of life 5,000 years ago. This means that our picture of Neolithic life and society is unusually complete here.

There is surprising variety in the landscape of Orkney. The first impression of gentle uniformity disintegrates as one gets to know the islands; hills and moorland, bogs, steep-sided valleys, cliffs and beaches all reveal themselves. All of the larger islands have some high ground and moorland as well as fertile lowlands, but Hoy stands out by virtue of its steep topography. The hills of Hoy dominate the Orkney landscape from many aspects and, as we shall see, they may well have had a deeper spiritual significance in prehistory. The steeper countryside of Hoy reflects a difference in the underlying geology. Ancient volcanic activity here resulted in hard igneous rocks overlying the sandstones in some places, and minerals such as iron are to be found (Figure 5).

Orkney does not have the geological diversity of its northern neighbour, Shetland, but there are places where earlier rocks can still be found. Around Stromness there are granites and gneisses which once protruded above the tropical seas as a range of low islands. Associated mineral deposits in this area include copper and uranium, though Orkney is not generally mineral rich.

Environment and setting

The fragmented and low-lying nature of the Orkney archipelago means that the two main influences on life are – and have always been – the winds that cross the islands and the waters that surround them. Even today life is constrained by the state of the tide and the strength of the wind. Their influence was even stronger in the past, as the monuments of World Heritage Orkney show.

Orkney today provides a setting that belies its tropical past – as one of the most northerly parts of the British Isles it is but a small island group off a larger island group on the north-west fringes of Europe. It lies at latitude 59° north and this means that winter days are short, though they lengthen rapidly in the spring to provide almost continuous daylight around midsummer. The climate is mild, but generally cool and dominated by the wind. There is plentiful rain. Vegetation today is low-lying and scrubby, and trees are stunted and rare.

Five thousand years ago, in the Neolithic, trees were more abundant. Ancient pollen from deep within Orcadian bogs has shown that species such as hazel and birch were relatively common.[2] Orcadian soils are fertile and the natural landscape was rich in many species, but it was also open to exploitation by the early farmers, who unwittingly started the process of long-term degradation by the wind when they cleared the woodland for their crops and animals. There is evidence of intensive manuring from early on and the farmers were able to maintain the fertility of the land by building up soils, but they found it harder to replace the shelter of the trees. Only in recent times have patches of woodland reappeared, with careful shelter belt management and the use of artificial wind-breaks.

Farming first came to Orkney about 5,500 years ago. At that time the climate showed all the traits with which we are familiar today, but the farmer's life was never easy. People had to work hard to produce a successful harvest and yet maintain the fertility of their land, and they lived under the constant threat of failure. In summer the long hours of daylight added to the carefully managed routines of farming to provide an intensive boost to the crops and pastures. Harvests could be rich. Excessive rain, or a cold snap, however, could easily bring a premature end to the growing season and in these years starvation loomed over the islanders. In a very real sense the early inhabitants of Orkney had to maintain an uneasy truce with the natural elements. This helped to endow the elements with a physical, tangible presence in the eyes of the early Orcadians.

The land was not the only source of resources for the early inhabitants of Orkney. The seas around the islands are shallow and rich, affected by warm

FIGURE 4 (*above*).
Sandstone cliffs in
Orkney. The bedding
planes of the sandstone
are clearly visible.
RAYMOND PARKS

FIGURE 5 (*left*).
St John's Head in Hoy.
RAYMOND PARKS

MAP 2.
Orkney, with the
locations of the
World Heritage Sites.
KENNY SWINNEY

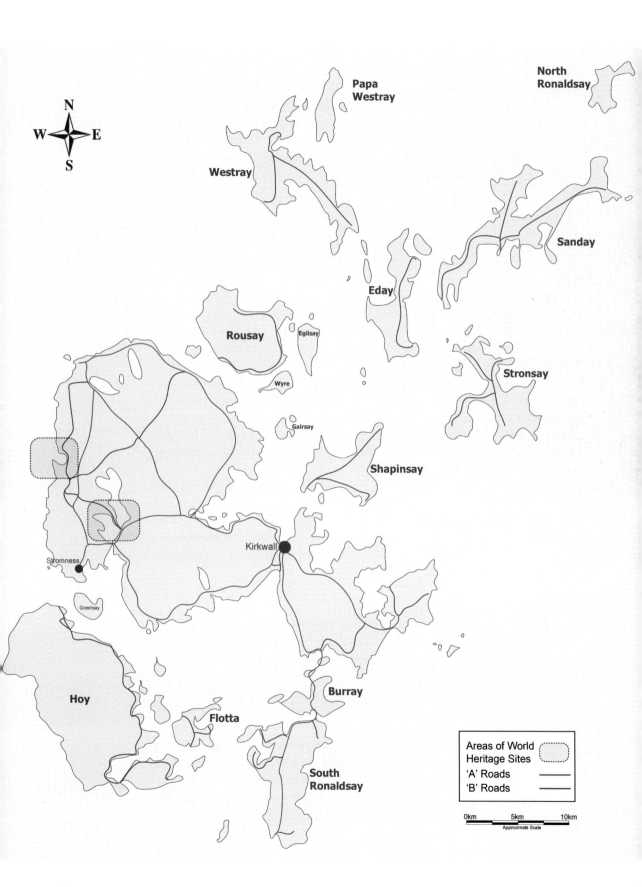

N
W E
S

North
Ronaldsay

Papa
Westray

Westray

Sanday

Rousay

Egilsay

Eday

Wyre

Stronsay

Gairsay

Shapinsay

Kirkwall

Stromness

Graemsay

Hoy

Burray

Flotta

South
Ronaldsay

Areas of World
Heritage Sites
'A' Roads
'B' Roads

0km   5km   10km
Approximate Scale

ocean currents which increase productivity. In most places access to the sea was relatively easy and safe, and boats could be drawn up to shelter from the ravages of the winter storms. A variety of fish, shellfish, sea mammals and birds, as well as plant-life, was available from the Orkney waters, and provided vital proteins and fats to supplement the diet of the farmers. The sea also acted as a vital means of communication, keeping Orkney at the centre of a network of routeways that ensured it did not become peripheral. In later times this network extended from Ireland to Scandinavia.

The World Heritage Sites

There are five components to the Heart of Neolithic Orkney: the settlement site of Skara Brae (Figure 6); the stone circle, henge, adjacent standing stone and burial mounds at the Ring of Brodgar; the stone circle and henge at the Stones of Stenness; the stone settings known as the Watch Stone and the Barnhouse Stone; and the chambered tomb of Maeshowe.

All were in use around 5,000 years ago, and they are, of course, only part of the world of Neolithic Orkney. There are many other Neolithic sites across the islands. Over time their fate has differed; for example, Skara Brae lay hidden from view for several millennia, while the stones of Brodgar and Stenness remained a visible part of the landscape. The sites did not go out of mind just because their primary use had changed, however. Each has played an active role over the years, including their place today as well-visited heritage sites, stimulating centres of research, and a magnet that attracts thousands of visitors to Orkney every year (Map 2).

These sites are unique by virtue of their good preservation and the fact that together they provide an astonishingly complete glimpse of life in the past. All too often archaeologists have to deal with but one element of the world of prehistory: they may have burial sites but no settlements, or ritual sites but no burials. Orkney is unusual in that a combination of interlocking evidence has survived.

Skara Brae

Skara Brae comprises the remains of at least nine stone-built structures, most of which have been interpreted as houses. Each house leads off an inter-connecting, covered passageway which allowed the inhabitants to move between different parts of the settlement without going into the open. This may have been useful during the bleak Orcadian winter, though it is likely that the people of Skara Brae spent much of their time outside throughout the rest of the year (Figure 7).

Like most villages today, Skara Brae was inhabited over a considerable period, probably about 600 years. Houses were added and modified throughout that time, and some fell out of use. The earliest buildings were constructed about 3100 BC though, intriguingly, they made use of midden material from an earlier, as yet unidentified, settlement that is likely to have lain close by. Skara Brae flourished in the years between 2900 and 2600 BC, but by 2500 BC it had apparently been abandoned.

The earlier houses at Skara Brae were freestanding, while the later buildings were tightly interlocked around the passageways. In general the house pattern was very uniform, though there are some differences between the earlier and later buildings. Although the earlier buildings do not survive above two or three courses of stone, some of the later structures apparently stand to roof height. The houses were built of thick stone walls which incorporated midden material – rotted-down rubbish that takes on a thick sticky consistency. Not only did this help to stabilize the walls, it made an excellent insulation which would have been especially important during the cold Orcadian winters.

The average Skara Brae house comprised a single large room with rounded corners. At its heart was the hearth, bounded by low stone slabs and with plenty of room to move on all sides. At the centre of one wall was a single, low, entrance door with a bolt on the inside. Ahead of the door, through the smoke from the fire, the most striking feature of the room was a large stone dresser set against the opposite wall and comprising three shelves each divided into two bays. On either side of the hearth, slabs set on edge defined bed spaces which would have been filled with seaweed and furs, and there were usually small shelves set into the walls at the head of each bed. In the earlier houses the beds were set into recesses in the walls, in later houses they project into the room. Other features of the room included stone tanks set into the floor by the dresser, grinding stones, and possible rubbish areas. In addition, each house had at least one cell set into the thickness of the wall. Some of the cells have drains which lead away from them and these are likely to have functioned as lavatories.

The use of stone at Skara Brae means that the remains are remarkably well preserved, but the preservation goes further than that. In addition to the walls and furnishings a happy combination of sandy soils and dampness has led to the survival of much of the ephemera of everyday life. The stone flakes and blades that made up an important part of the Stone Age tool kit are well known from other sites, as are the broken sherds of pottery, but at Skara Brae these are joined by a wide range of bone tools as well as artefacts of whalebone and pumice. Some are heavy tools such as mattocks and shovels; others are more delicate, such as pins and needles. Small perforated bones have been interpreted as whistles for dogs. In addition, there are many pieces of jewellery, including both finished and unfinished beads, as well as vegetable matter, such as puff balls, that are likely to have been medicinal, and bindings, made from heather root. The artefactual debris from Skara Brae is supplemented by ecofactual material that tells us about the environment. This includes unworked animal and fish bone as well as shells, all of which throws light on lifestyle and diet some 5,000 years ago (Figure 8).

One house at Skara Brae, though part of the later settlement, stands apart from the other buildings and may have served a different purpose. House 8 incorporates many structural differences and these have led to its interpretation as some sort of workshop. It is the only building with an entrance porch; inside, there is none of the usual furniture, no beds or dresser, but there are many niches and recesses in the walls. There is no cell, but there is a central hearth as well as a flue arrangement leading through the wall opposite the door. When it was excavated by Gordon Childe and

FIGURE 7 (*right*).
Skara Brae: general view.
C. WICKHAM-JONES

MAP 3.
Skara Brae and the other archaeological sites around the Bay of Skaill.
KENNY SWINNEY

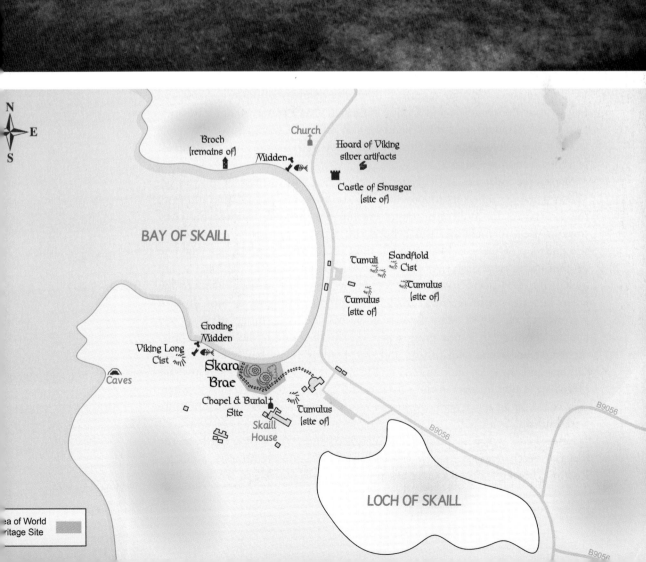

N E S

Broch
(remains of)

Church

Hoard of Viking
silver artifacts

Midden

Castle of Snusgar
(site of)

BAY OF SKAILL

Tumuli

Sandfield
Cist

Tumulus
(site of)

Tumulus
(site of)

Eroding
Midden

Viking Long
Cist

Skara
Brae

Caves

Chapel & Burial
Site

Tumulus
(site of)

Skaill
House

B9056

B9056

LOCH OF SKAILL

Area of World
Heritage Site

B9056

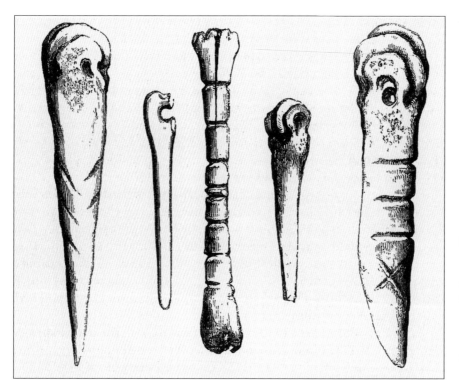

FIGURE 8.
A nineteenth-century
engraving of some of
the bone objects from
Skara Brae. Preservation
like this is rare in
Scottish archaeology.
Of particular interest is
the central bone, which
has been notched to
make beads but never
finished (from Wilson
1863, *Prehistoric Annals
of Scotland*).

his team in the 1920s they remarked upon the quantity of pottery sherds and flaked stone debris inside and Childe suggested that a stone worker had operated here.[3] Although it is difficult to be sure so many years after the original work, it does seem likely that this building may have played a specialized role in the community (Map 3).

Skara Brae today lies at the edge of the sea, but this was not so in the past. When it was occupied it is likely that the sea lay some two or three miles to the west. Over the millennia coastal erosion has gradually worked the coast towards the settlement and this process still takes place today, very much on the doorstep of the site. Skara Brae is now protected by a thick sea wall and its continuing protection over time is an ongoing problem for the body which looks after it, Historic Scotland. It is possible that some of the settlement has fallen into the sea in recent centuries, though archaeologists do not think it was ever much larger. Skara Brae is likely to have been home to some 100 people who lived in family groups, farmed the surrounding land and supplemented their harvest with fishing and wild-fowling. They had contacts across Orkney and the great monuments at Brodgar and Stenness are likely to have played an important part in their lives, as did tombs such as Maeshowe, where they could get in touch with the ancestors and where some of the community were buried.

Since its discovery in the mid nineteenth century, Skara Brae has been the focus of much research, mostly centred around its interpretation as a village. Recently, however, David Clarke has argued that it is possible to see Skara Brae in different ways:[4] as a village; as a secular centre with a few privileged inhabitants who received tribute from surrounding communities; as a religious centre whose inhabitants received offerings; and as the home of a community of artisans who exchanged their skills for the necessities of everyday life. These are all plausible explanations; some develop the ideas of others such as Euan MacKie, who has looked in particular at the suggestion that Skara Brae was the home of a religious elite.[5] Nevertheless, in this publication Skara Brae is seen as an ordinary, common-or-garden village. The primary reason for this lies in the number of similar sites to be found around Orkney. Skara Brae is by no means alone; other stone-built 'villages' from this time include Rinyo in Rousay, Barnhouse in Mainland, Pool in Sanday, Noltland in Westray, and Howmae in North Ronaldsay. While it is always nice to think that we might have discovered something quite out of the ordinary, it is far more likely that we are looking at the remains of everyday life. Furthermore, if we consider our own lives, it is quite possible that these explanations are not mutually exclusive. Many settlements today contain both religious and secular personnel, as well as specialized artisans. Life is rarely as compartmentalized as some archaeologists would make it.

Life at Skara Brae seems to have become more difficult as encroaching sands reduced the fertility of the surrounding fields. By 2500 BC the village had been abandoned. Most of the houses were at least partially emptied of their contents before this happened, but house 7 went on in use even after it had been partly filled with sand. The final deposits here are quite strange: the skull of a bull lay in one bed; a bone dish full of red, ochre, pigment lay on the floor; and there was a cache of jewellery in the cell. Two burials were found, which may have been inserted towards the end of its use.

Where did the people from Skara Brae go? We cannot answer that precisely, but it may not have been far away. If the settlement fell out of use gradually, as people found it increasingly difficult to cultivate the sand-filled fields, then new settlement may have arisen on a piecemeal basis. Ironically, we know less about domestic life and houses in Orkney in the periods after the great stone settlements of the Neolithic had been abandoned. In some ways everyday life went on with few changes into the following period, the Bronze Age, with the obvious exception that metal goods were introduced, though they may not have been common. In other ways there were considerable changes: settlement seems to have been more dispersed and, as the result of a greater emphasis placed on the individual, there were far-reaching changes in burial practice and other rituals.

The Ring of Brodgar

The Ring of Brodgar comprises a circle of sixty stones on a platform inside a circular ditch (Figure 9). Sites like this, made up of a central platform inside a ditch, often with an exterior bank, are known today as henges and they were built right across Britain during the Neolithic. We have no idea what they would have been called when they were in use. Henges seem to have

FIGURE 9.
View of the Ring of
Brodgar.
RAYMOND PARKS

FIGURE 10.
View of the Stones of
Stenness.
RAYMOND PARKS

functioned as ceremonial sites. Many, as at Brodgar, were enhanced by the erection of a circle of standing stones. At the Ring of Brodgar the platform is 104 m in diameter and the ditch would originally have been about 6 m wide and 3 m deep. Thirty-six of the stones still stand, though some have been re-erected, and others have been reduced to stumps. Around the outside of the ring, a complex of burial mounds has grown up comprising 13 mounds, some of which are very impressive, and there is a small stone setting, known as the Comet Stone. Brodgar lies on a narrow neck of land that juts between the Loch of Harray and the Loch of Stenness; it is a spectacular location, shared with a whole series of ceremonial sites from the same period, though it is likely that the loch waters were slightly lower, and thus further away, when it was originally built.

Even today, despite the monument's somewhat eroded state, it is possible to get an idea of the great effort that must have gone into designing and building it. The ditch is cut into the underlying bedrock, which was no mean feat for people who had to rely on stone and bone tools. The stones that stand

MAP 4.
The archaeology of the Brodgar peninsula.
KENNY SWINNEY

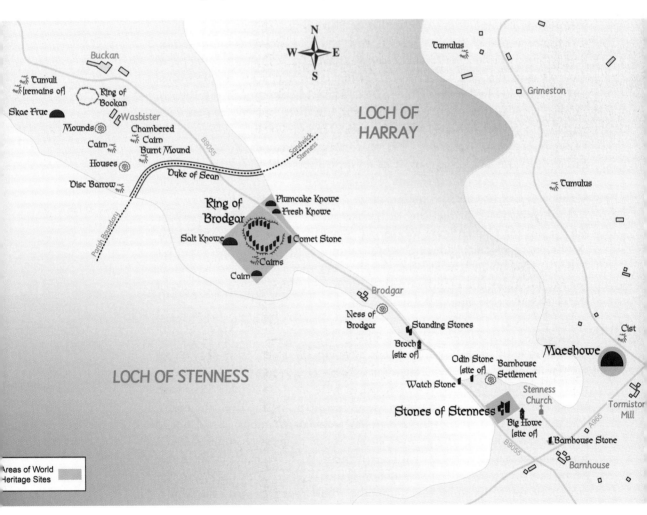

13

to their original height reach between 2 and 4.5 m high. Considering that each must have considerable 'roots' of a metre or more of stone below ground level, it is possible to appreciate the skills that have gone into quarrying, transporting and erecting them. In recent years Colin Richards has investigated a stone quarry at Vestrafiold, above Skara Brae, from which some stones may have been cut,[6] and Nick Card has identified two possible submerged standing stones lying by the shore of the loch, not far from the site, perhaps the result of a prehistoric mishap.[7] Moreover, the construction of a site like the Ring of Brodgar did not just involve physical effort. There was the site to choose, the circle to draw out, stones to quarry, transport and erect. The builders were able to make use of the natural fracturing properties of the local stone, not only in the sheer presence of the monoliths, but also in their aspect. Most have slanting tops and these have been carefully set, both here and at the Stones of Stenness, in order to complement each other and add to the natural viewpoints apparent in the surrounding landscape.

The Ring of Brodgar as we see it was built sometime between 2500 and 2000 BC. It is likely to have been a communal effort that involved many surrounding communities, such as that at Skara Brae. There were no doubt ceremonies as part of the construction work and, just like many of our monuments today, work may never quite have stopped here. The surrounding burial mounds show that this was a most important place and many people wished to be buried in close reach of the stones. Today, the interior of the Ring of Brodgar is a blank, heather-covered platform, but there are likely to have been various settings of timber and hearths within the stone circle, as seen at the Stones of Stenness. Archaeology has yet to reveal the secrets of Brodgar, and perhaps they are best left as part of its mystery. Even today a visit to the Ring of Brodgar is a special experience for many people, enhanced by the wild setting and lack of intrusive interpretation.

To the south-west of the Ring of Brodgar, and within the World Heritage Site, stands the Comet Stone, which is 1.75 m tall. It stands on a small platform some 14 m across and there are also stumps of two other stones here. We know nothing about their original purpose, but they are likely to have been erected in conjunction with the work at the Ring of Brodgar as a vital part of the ceremonies that took place there (Map 4).

The Stones of Stenness and adjacent stones
Like the Ring of Brodgar, the Stones of Stenness comprise a circle of standing stones, but on a smaller scale (Figure 10). There were 12 stones at Stenness, of which four still stand, set on a platform that lay inside a circular ditch with an exterior bank. A single causeway crosses the ditch, leading from the north. The ditch and bank as they are seen today are reconstructions carried out as part of excavation and display work in the 1970s, as Stenness suffered much from damage caused in the early nineteenth century. The tenant farmer in this period saw the Stones of Stenness as a hindrance to agriculture and was in the process of using dynamite to remove the stones when he was, thankfully,

stopped. To this day the holes drilled to receive the charges may still be seen in one of the largest stones.

The Stones of Stenness is older than the Ring of Brodgar; it is thought that its construction began about 3000 BC. The surviving stones rise to a height of 5.7 m and they have been carefully set so that their sloping tops provide a frame that mirrors the outline of the hills of Hoy, some 10 km to the south-west. The sheer size of the stones suggests that they may have been erected on a more open space, before the surrounding ditch and bank were built. Inside the circle there seem to have been other, complex, settings. Excavation across a section of the interior in the 1970s revealed a series of pits and post holes as well as a large central hearth, though not all of these features were necessarily in use at the same time. It is thought that the Stones of Stenness continued in use for several centuries; much later, in the early twentieth century, a group of low stones was reconstructed into an 'altar', though the horizontal slab of this has since been displaced.

As at the Ring of Brodgar, the construction of the Stones of Stenness was a skilled job that required considerable effort, probably from several communities. Not only are the stones of great size, but the ditch itself was 7 m wide and over 2 m deep, and was cut into bedrock. Work in the 1980s uncovered a substantial stone-built village in the field adjacent to the stones, at Barnhouse, by the shore of the Loch of Harray. Some of the settings within the stones are mirrored in the design of the village, which is likely to have been closely associated with its monumental neighbour. It has even been suggested that the hearth at the centre of the Stones of Stenness may have been moved from the largest of the structures at Barnhouse, where the empty slots from identical hearth stones were recently discovered. It may well be that the first activity at the Stones of Stenness centred on a ceremonial structure or house, not unlike the larger structures at Barnhouse. The ditch, platform and stones with which we associate the site today may have been a later development.

Also included within the World Heritage designation are two isolated standing stones: the Watch Stone and the Barnhouse Stone. The Watch Stone stands on the south shore of the break where the Loch of Stenness runs into the Loch of Harray. Today it lies right beside the road, at one end of the causeway over to the Brodgar peninsula. The Watch Stone stands some 5.5 m tall and was originally part of other stone settings between the Ring of Brodgar and the Stones of Stenness. The Barnhouse Stone, 3 m tall, stands in a field at the south end of the peninsula, to the south-west of Maeshowe. Today it stands alone, but it is likely to have been part of a more elaborate complex in the past.

Maeshowe

Maeshowe comprises one of the largest burial mounds of Neolithic Europe (Figure 11). The mound itself is covered with turf; it is 35 m across and over 7 m high. It covers a central stone-built chamber with three side cells and

a single entrance passage some 11 m long. The tomb sits on a flat circular platform with a surrounding ditch and bank.

The interior chamber measures just over 2 m by 2 m, and originally stood about 5 m high. In common with the other monuments of Neolithic Orkney, it is built of slabs, incorporating some massive stones. Each side chamber is roofed with a single flagstone, for example, while the individual stones that line the entrance passage weigh up to 3 tonnes each. At each corner of the main chamber stands a huge upright slab, and Euan MacKie has suggested that, prior to the building of the monument, these were free-standing stones in the open air.[8] The three side cells lie some 80 cm above the floor of the main chamber. Each could apparently be closed off with its own blocking stone. Three large chunky stones now lie on the floor of the main chamber at the entrance to the individual cells.

One fascinating feature of Maeshowe is the way in which it is aligned

FIGURE II.
View of Maeshowe.
SIGURD TOWRIE

FIGURE 12.
James Farrer drew the interior of Maeshowe as he found it in the nineteenth century. The entry hole in the roof shows clearly, as do the Viking runes.
COURTESY OF THE ORKNEY LIBRARY AND ARCHIVE PHOTOGRAPHIC LIBRARY

INTERIOR VIEW OF MAESHOWE.

towards the setting sun at midwinter. For a few days on either side of the winter solstice the setting sun shines directly along the passage to light the main chamber and the cell opposite the entrance. Similar alignments have been observed at other Neolithic sites, such as Newgrange in Ireland, where the passage is lined up with the midwinter solstice. The sun and stars must have played an important role in Neolithic society as they marked the passing of the seasons and so they may well have figured in wider local beliefs. The builders of Maeshowe must have calculated the direction for the passage very carefully and in this respect the positioning of four standing stones prior to the building of the mound would have been an important step in getting the right alignment.

The platform and ditch at Maeshowe are reminiscent of henge sites such as the Ring of Brodgar, leading to a theory that the site originally comprised a ceremonial centre. Support for this was provided in 1996 when excavations directed by Colin Richards as part of Historic Scotland's management of the site uncovered the empty socket for a large standing stone on the platform beyond the mound.[9] Colin also revealed that there was originally a substantial stone wall bounding the ditch, but this had collapsed not long after construction and had since been enhanced by turf and rubble.[10]

Maeshowe was built around 2500 BC. By the time it was entered by Farrer in 1861[11] the chamber was empty, but evidence from other Neolithic tombs shows that among other things they were built to house the bones of the dead. The quantity of bones varies considerably between sites: some seem to have held most of a community while others may have held only certain individuals, but in general these were communal resting places that are likely to have been identified with a specific community. We do not know exactly where the builders and users of Maeshowe lived, but given its proximity to the ceremonial sites of the Brodgar peninsula it is likely to have been an important part of the religious activity that took place here.

Maeshowe is also famous today for more recent activity on site (Figure 12). In the mid twelfth century AD it was broken into by Norsemen on more than one occasion. One group sheltered in the tomb during a thunderstorm. In common with bored youth everywhere, these later users of the tomb left their mark: the stone walls of the chamber at Maeshowe are covered by graffiti in the form of runic messages. These messages vary in content from the boastful to the frankly pornographic,[12] but one curious passage suggests that a considerable amount of treasure was removed. This is puzzling because metal was unknown in the Neolithic, but has been thought by some to suggest that the tomb was adapted to be the burial site for a Viking noble in later times. Colin Richards' excavations of 1996 provided incidental support for this with evidence that the bank surrounding the platform had been rebuilt in the ninth century AD. The runes at Maeshowe comprise the largest collection of runes outside of Scandinavia and they are an important study resource for academics – perhaps a salutary lesson for those who would remove all painted graffiti from our townscape walls today!

Other sites in the area

World Heritage Sites are designated under very strict criteria, and though the immediate vicinity of the monuments detailed above includes several other Neolithic sites these were not included within the designation for various reasons. These remains will be described and discussed later on, but it is important to note their existence here, because they all form part of the great ceremonial centre that lay along the Ness of Brodgar. Perhaps the most important of these are the settlement of Barnhouse by the Stones of Stenness and the henge and mounds at Bookan to the north-west of the Ring of Brodgar. Ongoing research in the area still adds to the list of archaeological material here; in 2003 further Neolithic structures were recorded at Ness of Brodgar to the south-east of the Ring of Brodgar.[13] Work in 2004 suggested that these may include a chambered tomb[14] and there have been suggestions that the many isolated standing stones that survive formed part of an avenue, or other linear feature, that linked the various ceremonial monuments.[15]

Not surprisingly, there are also later sites in the area. Bronze Age houses and mounds at Wasbister, between Bookan and the Ring of Brodgar, attest to building activity while the earlier monuments were probably still in use as active centres. To the south-east of the Stones of Stenness lies Big Howe, an Iron Age broch site that is clearly in a significant position at the head of the two lochs and which may well have made use of redundant stones from the earlier monuments. The Dyke of Sean, which runs across the peninsula to the north of the Ring of Brodgar, may be medieval in origin (though there is a suggestion that it goes back to the Bronze Age), and there is possible medieval activity associated with Stenness Church at the south end of the peninsula. The Ness of Brodgar has been an important place through time, right up to the present day and the assignation of World Heritage Status.

Archaeology across Orkney

Orkney is famous for its archaeology. Well-preserved sites from the Neolithic onwards abound across the islands, and the World Heritage Sites are thus a small part of a much greater whole. The reasons for their selection are discussed below (Chapter Twelve); for now it is enough to note that together they provide a glimpse of Neolithic life that is both remarkably detailed and unusually complete, comprising as it does elements of everyday life, of ceremony, and of burial. It is most unusual to get this sort of sweeping view, especially in such a small area. It is also important, however, to set these sites into their wider context, both at the time of occupation and through more recent times. Neolithic Orkney was a sophisticated place, and it is possible that the sites of the Ness of Brodgar formed a special heartland for the Neolithic communities of the islands. They did not disappear from view at the end of the Neolithic, however, and it is likely that this special role continued, albeit in different ways, into more recent times. Certainly, once written records abound, from the nineteenth century on, there is plentiful evidence of the importance of this place, in the form of engravings and other visual depictions. The sites that make up the Heart of Neolithic Orkney are especially important for those who live among them and elsewhere across Orkney, but their significance is wider than that. They draw many visitors to Orkney both from Britain and from further afield. Those who cannot visit in person make good use of the many websites, such as www.orkneyjar.com or www.maeshowe.co.uk.

At the beginning of the twenty-first century the importance of these archaeological sites has swung full circle and the monuments of the Brodgar peninsula are once again active centres of pilgrimage. They are promoted around the world both in their own right, and as iconic of Orkney in general. Heritage has become an important element of modern society and the varied components of the Heart of Neolithic Orkney are an essential part of this.

CHAPTER TWO

The People Before: Mesolithic Orkney

....

Background

The World Heritage Sites in Orkney are inscribed as Neolithic sites. That is to say they relate to the time, some 5,000 years ago, immediately after the introduction of farming to Orkney. There were people in the islands prior to this, however, and in order to understand the Neolithic and its monuments it is important to understand life in the islands before this period.

Before the introduction of farming, life in Scotland was based around hunting, gathering and fishing, and this period is known archaeologically as the Mesolithic. Little is known about Mesolithic Orkney because, unlike the later inhabitants of the islands, the people of the Mesolithic did not build stone monuments, nor did they live in permanent houses. Mesolithic sites do not comprise upstanding stone remains, and they can be hard to find.

The Mesolithic lifestyle

The Mesolithic lifestyle was geared to mobility and this affected the nature of their settlements. People lived in small communities, probably based around an extended family including immediate uncles and aunts as well as children and grandparents, but they did not stay in the same place all the year round, and they may well not have always been with the same group. Communities split and reformed as some people left to travel and exploit the resources of different parts of the land and sea-scape at different times of the year. These splits may well have been related to gender and age in a way that might seem alien to us. Thus groups of adolescents may have travelled to the rivers and lochs to fish, men may have gone to the uplands to hunt, and women and children worked to harvest the woodlands for roots, nuts and berries. Some areas demanded smaller sections of society, others could support larger mixed settlements. The coast, for example, might provide work for everyone as there were shellfish to gather and process, fish, sea mammals and birds to hunt, and other resources like stones to gather as raw materials from the beach. Different tasks were undertaken at different places.

The Mesolithic community had to find all that it needed from the local environment and this involved a regular round of work: there were hides to process and stitch; stone and bones to flake into shape; foodstuffs to preserve; shelters to maintain; and roots and withies to weave into baskets and bindings. The most important need apart from food was the daily requirement to collect fuel for the fire; this involved exploiting different parts of the woodlands, since individual woods were collected for their various properties: old damp logs to smoke food; resinous pine for protection through the night; or dry tinder for a hot fire on which to cook.[1] As fuel became scarce in any one place, so the community had to think about moving on.

Mesolithic remains

The fluid Mesolithic lifestyle was reflected in people's belongings. Everything had to be packed and carried. Even shelters used elements such as poles and skin coverings that were easily obtainable or transportable. Much was based on organic materials such as bone, hide, and wood and sadly, in the millennia since the Mesolithic, the acid soils of Scotland have worked to dissolve away most of the evidence. In many places the only signs that people once lived here, some 8,000 years ago, are handfuls of sharp stone flakes, patches of charcoal and burnt hazelnut shell, a few nondescript pits, and (if we are really lucky), the traces of post holes where poles were once set into the ground to support a structure.

Unlike the later inhabitants of Scotland, the Mesolithic communities did not build lasting ceremonial and ritual centres. This is not to say that their lives were devoid of any spiritual element; research has highlighted the spiritual importance of natural places and forces for many peoples, and this is likely to have been the case in the Mesolithic.[2] After the Ice Age, Scotland had no shortage of landmarks on which to base a relationship between the people and their community of gods or spirits. Many of these would be familiar to us today: isolated rocks; spectacular crags; or steep waterfalls. Others have disappeared: particular trees; pasture-filled clearings; or transient sand-bars. And these were not necessarily restricted to physical places: thunderstorms, high winds, and the aurora borealis, for example, were all features of the environment to which people could relate. A further dimension may well have been provided by events such as floods, with which we are still familiar today, or minor earthquakes which, though unfamiliar to Scotland's present population, were a common occurrence in the millennia immediately after the last Ice Age.

It is thus impossible to recognise many of the places which were known and revered by our Mesolithic ancestors, but that does not mean they did not exist. There is ample evidence for a flourishing Mesolithic society across Scotland and increasing evidence that this included Orkney. The places that were important to these people have long been forgotten, but it is not hard to imagine how the landscape once looked, especially when we get further away from the towns and cities of the early twenty-first century.

Finding Mesolithic sites

In times past, when people worked the land with horses and walked the same ground year after year, stone tools were frequently found as witness to the people who had gone before and the evidence from these finds included the Mesolithic. In recent years, as farming has become mechanised and the pace of development has speeded up, it is increasingly difficult for people to spot these ephemeral traces. Today, archaeology is recognised as an important part of the nation's heritage, and various steps have been taken to ensure that remains are recognised, evaluated, studied where necessary, and even preserved on occasion. Archaeology is now an integral part of the planning process and provides opportunities for new sites to be recognised in advance of developments such as building, roads and forestry.[3]

This has had little impact on Mesolithic remains, however. If anything, it has worked against their discovery. Mesolithic remains are not only hard to find in today's mechanised world, but in addition, pre-development archaeological evaluations tend to focus on upstanding archaeological remains. As Mesolithic sites lie below the ground, this counts against them. Nevertheless, new Mesolithic sites are still found, but in Orkney they are rare – though while this book was being written, one was discovered in the course of fieldwalking by Miriam Cantley from the University of York (Figure 13).

The physical remains of Mesolithic Orkney

For many years it was assumed that Orkney was uninhabited during the Mesolithic period, but recently people have recognised that Mesolithic remains do exist here. However, they are, as yet, few and far between and they have been little studied. One reason for the lack of archaeological work on Mesolithic Orkney is the exceptional quality of the later remains to be found in the islands. From at least the eighteenth century onwards visitors to Orkney have been fascinated by the ancient remains, and these remains have for many years been incorporated into academic work.[4] The sites of the Neolithic and later periods in Orkney have been recorded by pioneering photographers and surveyors, and they were incorporated into mainstream interpretations of the development of society in Britain as a whole. This process increased in momentum from the 1960s with the development of new schools of archaeological theory and the introduction of new techniques to make sense of the remains of the past. The quality and quantity of material from Neolithic Orkney meant that it has come to play a central role in developing ideas about the past. From the 1970s to the present day, archaeological excavation has played an important role in Orkney and produced increasing amounts of data for analysis. In some cases the quantity of data has meant that site reports have yet to be published, but this does not mean that archaeological interest in the islands has waned.

Unlike the Neolithic, Mesolithic Orkney is represented only by a few

FIGURE 13.
Test pitting to find the
remains of Mesolithic
Orkney in Stronsay in
1990 (nothing to find
here!).

C. WICKHAM-JONES

isolated collections of worked stone, and until recently these have been largely overlooked in most considerations of the prehistory of the islands. The paucity of the material from this period has in itself led to a failure to search for new Mesolithic remains in Orkney, as archaeologists 'knew' that Mesolithic material did not occur here. Only recently has there been a change in the direction of study. Mesolithic Orkney is now accepted as an important research topic in relation to our understanding of the World Heritage Sites in Orkney, and it is starting to appear once again as a topic in research grant applications.

There are, in 2005, 20 sites where Mesolithic-type stone tools have been found in Orkney. Most were found during farming activities and to date none of the sites has produced good Mesolithic remains apart from the tools. None has been excavated under modern conditions, and in many cases the setting or context of the stone tools has long since been destroyed. The discovery of Mesolithic tools in the makeup of the Bronze Age cairn at Long Howe during work by Orkney Archaeological Trust in August 2004 is very exciting because it offers the possibility that Mesolithic features might have survived below the cairn.[5] Archaeological work to test this hypothesis is planned for the summer of 2006 (Figure 14).

Other evidence for Mesolithic Orkney

The physical remains of Mesolithic Orkney tell us little beyond the fact that people lived in the islands prior to the Neolithic. There are other ways, however, in which we may be able to flesh out the picture. The first of these is, perhaps, human nature: the Mesolithic settlement of Scotland extended to the north coast.[6] From that point the islands of Orkney would have been visible, and to skilled sea-farers such as those of the Mesolithic, the crossing, while difficult, would not have been impossible. The archipelago offered a rich environment to its early inhabitants. Recent palaeoenvironmental work has shown the development of locally mixed woodland vegetation[7] and this suggests the presence of various animals and birds. The local seas and lochs were productive and there were plenty of other resources such as fresh water and stone for tools. It is unthinkable that people did not cross the Pentland Firth to make use of the plentiful resources they would find here.

Moreover, the recent discovery of traces of a timber house during excavations led by Colin Richards at Wideford Hill in 2003[8] opens up the possibility that timber buildings were constructed in Orkney in the past, and that

FIGURE 14.
The site of the
Mesolithic finds on
Long Howe in 2004.
ORKNEY
ARCHAEOLOGICAL
TRUST

archaeological remains may have been preserved. It was often assumed that there was a general lack of timber for building in Orkney throughout prehistory and this has hampered recent investigation of the Orcadian Mesolithic. Furthermore, it seemed that even if wood had been used in ancient Orkney, its traces would not have survived. This is now known to be erroneous on two counts: timber *was* available, both as drift wood and as local, if scrubby, woodland; and evidence for timber buildings *can* survive. Richards' discovery of two timber buildings in close association with a stone building from the Early Neolithic is an important one. It is not the precise date of these buildings that is important (though it looks as if they are early), rather it is the indication that timber buildings were built in Orkney and that their traces can survive to the present day. This backs up the information from palaeobotanical studies that woodland – and thus timber of a size suitable for building – was once more abundant here[9] (Orkney today presents an almost treeless landscape). In this respect, it is important to remember that until now most archaeological excavation in Orkney has focused upon the discovery of stone structures; the excavation strategies may themselves have biased the evidence by working against the recovery of timber remains.

Additionally, sea level change means that many early sites in Orkney may have been lost. Across Scotland there has been considerable change in sea level since the end of the last Ice Age.[10] This has not been uniform around the country, but it is likely that the sea level in Orkney at the end of the Ice Age was as much as 30 m below its present levels. At present there is no detailed information on the rates of sea level change that have affected Orkney, but work is being done to remedy this. Sue Dawson, from St Andrews University, has been looking at the remains of small creatures known as diatoms, preserved in the sediments of both sea and loch.[11] The diatoms preserve a record that shows both the rise and fall of sea level: by taking cores of material from various sites it is possible to examine the changes from fresh water to marine diatoms, and once this change is dated it is possible to see when and how sea level has changed. By combining this information with other data we can construct maps of how the land has changed since the end of the Ice Age. Recent advances in underwater prospection will then help us to look for sites. With the use of Geographical Information Systems it is possible to predict the likely locations of Mesolithic remains underwater, by compiling information on the spread of known sites from a variety of comparable areas such as Norway and the west coast of Scotland. This is something that is currently under development by a team lead by Penny Spikins from York University.

Following on from this, we can go further afield for information on Mesolithic Orkney. There is increasing study of the early settlement of coastal areas at high latitudes. Research as far afield as Norway, Tierra del Fuego and Alaska has provided an interesting picture; and Orkney fits well into the pattern. Areas such as these provide a combination of factors that work together to encourage settlement: indented fjord-like coastlines and island archipelagos; providential currents and rich marine resources; safely accessible coasts and waters. It is no coincidence that many high latitude island groups have not only been settled from early on, but have seen flourishing coastal societies. There is no reason why Orkney should be different.

Finally, conceptual evidence for the Mesolithic in Orkney may be drawn from the nature of the Neolithic society in the islands. Archaeologists are agreed upon the amazing sophistication of the Neolithic culture that flourished here. The stone circles, burial mounds and stone-built villages (with their stone furnishings) are indeed amazing, but it is unlikely that they developed suddenly and out of nothing. Evidence for the Early Neolithic of Orkney is scanty but increasing. It too comprises stone-built structures, though as yet we know little about the precise way of life of these early farmers. How much of their culture was new? Domestic animals and crops, for example, did not exist in Orkney prior to the introduction of farming. They must have been brought to the islands and this must have involved the use of boats. Other elements of lifestyle are likely to have developed out of the pre-existing ways of the indigenous population. It is highly unlikely that monuments such as those of the later Neolithic could have arisen in a rootless, transient, society.

This is not just a question of physical ability, of the building and organization of the monuments: it is also a question of thoughts and feelings, of people's identification with the land. The Ness of Brodgar was clearly highly important to the local community, but why? The great monuments that stride along the narrow isthmus here indicate a society that had a deep and long-lived identification with the land. It is most likely that this identification goes well back into the pre-Neolithic, Mesolithic, times. Evidence elsewhere increasingly emphasizes the continuities between the Mesolithic and Neolithic in Scotland and Orkney is unlikely to have been any different.

Mesolithic Orkney – interpretation

The people of Mesolithic Orkney are likely to have arrived soon after the end of the Ice Age. There may have been only one family group, or perhaps there were several. They moved around the archipelago and some may only have visited the islands intermittently. They bought goods with them, including stone and bone tools and hides for shelter, but they also found plenty to make use of here. Orkney in the Mesolithic had much to offer but it was a very different land to that of today.

The primary differences in Orkney after the Ice Age lay in the lower sea levels and increased woodland. The land mass of the island group was bigger and the vegetation more varied. The early settlers needed boats to get to the islands, and boats were useful for transport, but the gentle topography meant that it was also possible to cross the land on foot. There were plentiful resources from land and sea, but it was not yet a stable environment. This was a time of great environmental change – perhaps not unlike today. The early peoples of Orkney had to cope both with short-term dramatic changes as the land settled after the Ice Age,[12] and with longer-term changes due to the ever changing patterns of global weather.[13] Sea levels rose rapidly in the first millennia after the Ice Age, and this would have been apparent to those who lived beside and harvested the coastal waters. Life would no doubt have become more arduous as the waters rose and familiar settlement sites and harvesting areas were flooded. To add to their trials there were frequent small earthquakes, some perhaps as much as force five on the Richter scale, as the land settled with the release of the weight of ice that had been forcing it down. Winter frost action led to land slips and scree slides. None of these were catastrophic, but they must have made life difficult; one wonders about their impact on local myths and stories.

In 6000 BC an event occurred which was truly catastrophic. An undersea landslide in the Storegga trench off the coast of Norway triggered a tsunami that reached proportions familiar today from events in Asia in December 2004.[14] The wave was probably some 15 m high when it hit Shetland, and it may not have been much lower in Orkney.[15] It would have been devastating for all who lived along the coast and the loss of life must have been considerable. This had serious implications for a small island community. Deposits that mark the trace of the wave have been found as far south as Berwick in the north of England, and it is likely that its effect continued further south. We know little about the precise impact of the Storegga tsunami in Orkney, but it is a sobering reminder that the British Isles are not as cosy and safe as we might think.

Longer-term changes to the climate included a slow drop in temperature. In the early years after the end of the Ice Age, temperatures were slightly warmer than those of today, but by the sixth millennium they had fallen. At this time there was also an increase in westerly winds and storm conditions which brought higher rainfall. As the land settled after the ice so localized events diminished, but more general changes continued.

As a result of this dynamic environment the Mesolithic inhabitants of Orkney may have been particularly receptive to transformation. They had to adapt. As their traditional ways of life became more difficult, so the introduction of new ways may have been welcomed rather than received with antipathy (as human nature might dictate). The introduction of farming must indeed have been an event of considerable significance to the local population and this would no doubt have contributed to their feelings about the land and their own place within it. The life of the farmer is very different to that of the hunter-fisher-gatherer; it demands a long-term and repeated input into a closely defined area of land, whereas the hunter often tends to range over a larger area and may only revisit places after a gap of several years. The adoption of farming tends to lead to more stable settlements and, though hunting rarely stops completely and people may still range widely on occasion, a close relationship of mutual responsibility tends to build up between a people and their home grounds.

From Mesolithic to Neolithic

Mesolithic Orkney offered a unique combination of instability within a rich environment, a mix which would catalyse the development of society with the arrival of farming. At the same time, there are clear signs that many aspects of the hunter-gatherer lifestyle did not disappear with the coming of the Neolithic. Some of the wild elements that were important in the Mesolithic, such as red deer, seem to have acquired increased significance even though the focus of everyday life had shifted to a reliance on farming and domestication. Excavation by David Clarke at the Neolithic settlement site of Links of Noltland in Westray has found evidence for the careful burial of whole carcasses of deer at the edge of the fields on the outside of the settlement site.[16] The Noltland deposits are also associated with the remains of fish, another Mesolithic staple that also turns up elsewhere on Neolithic sites, sometimes in large quantities. Shellfish are also common on many Neolithic sites: Orkney is famous for its Neolithic shell middens, which in many ways bear close resemblance to the Mesolithic shell middens found elsewhere in Scotland. There is also evidence for the harvesting of birds in Neolithic Orkney, but not only for food: bird bones were used in the manufacture of Neolithic jewellery.

Life in Neolithic Orkney had strong Mesolithic roots. It was about much

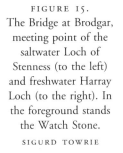

FIGURE 15.
The Bridge at Brodgar, meeting point of the saltwater Loch of Stenness (to the left) and freshwater Harray Loch (to the right). In the foreground stands the Watch Stone.

SIGURD TOWRIE

more than farming and building monuments. Wild resources played an important role. This is emphasized by one interpretation of Neolithic society which
envisages each local community operating under its own animal totem.[17] Some
of the individual chambered tombs have been found to contain assemblages of
specific animal bones and this has been interpreted as evidence for the use of
totemic spirits such as sea eagles (at the tomb of Isbister) or dogs (at Cuween).

The Mesolithic in the World Heritage Area

It is likely that the Brodgar isthmus was already significant to the Mesolithic
population of Orkney. The reasons behind this significance have yet to be
explored, but we know that the meeting point of the lochs offers a remarkable
combination of resources due to the influx of a rich freshwater loch (Harray)
with a tidal saltwater loch (Stenness) (Figure 15). Research on hunter-gatherer
societies elsewhere shows that particular combinations of land and sky are
often significant, together with other topographical features. The Brodgar
isthmus has many characteristics that would make it a significant natural place
in the way that is likely to have been important prior to the building of more
lasting monuments.

Precise Mesolithic information from the World Heritage area is scant,
though Mesolithic-type flints have been found in the locality at Barnhouse,
along the shores of the Loch of Stenness at Seatter, and at Wideford. To date,
excavations in the area have not targeted the Mesolithic, so that the known
finds come either from fieldwalking or are incidental finds from more recent
excavations. In 2005 a project undertaken by Miriam Cantley of the University
of York had the precise aim of looking for Mesolithic remains through fieldwalking and this has resulted in the discovery of one previously unknown
Mesolithic site, with very interesting stone tools, on the shores of the Loch of
Stenness at the Raga Shore. Evidence relating to the Mesolithic is clearly there,
though it has yet to be studied in depth.

CHAPTER THREE

The Arrival of Change:
The Early Neolithic

The end of the Mesolithic

By 4000 BC the Mesolithic inhabitants of Orkney were well settled into an annual routine that enabled them to exploit the resources of the islands to their best advantage. They had a comprehensive knowledge of the world in which they lived and may even have started to use this knowledge to improve the resource base available to them. By clearing vegetation, using controlled burning, or avoiding certain areas for periods of time they could encourage the growth of nuts or grasses, or provide enhanced browse for the wild game on which they depended. The Mesolithic way of life had provided everything that people needed for some 4,000 years, but the scene was set for change.

No one knows precisely why things changed; there are many theories that consider the pressures of increasing population, changes in the climate and resource base, and so on. Change was inevitable for Orkney because of its position at the north-western tip of Europe. The changes that led to the adoption of farming had been initiated around 9,000 years ago in the Near East and they rolled slowly westwards across Europe, developing momentum as they came.

The environment of fourth-millennium Orkney

It was not only life that settled down as people moved into the fourth millennium; the land too had stabilised. The upheavals of the first few millennia after the Ice Age had ended. Earthquakes were rare; sea level change had slowed. The islands were low and windswept, but they presented a very different aspect to that of today. Low woodland, including hazel, birch and other species, was well established across the landscape, albeit with frequent clearings and grassy moorland on the higher ground. The temperature was similar to that of today, though rainfall was gradually increasing. Inland areas of bog and marsh were common, but there was plenty of better-drained land to attract people looking for a home for their crops and animals.

The coast, as ever, was vulnerable to erosion and change. A slightly lower sea level, perhaps a metre or two below that of today, meant that the landmass was slightly bigger in area. There is evidence, for example, that Westray was

FIGURE 16.
Coring work along the
coast to look at
evidence for coastal
change.

C. WICKHAM-JONES

FIGURE 17.
The farmstead at the
Knap of Howar.

C. WICKHAM-JONES

joined to Papa Westray, while the deep indented bays of northern Sanday would not have existed. At the Bay of Skaill, on the west coast of Mainland Orkney, the coast is likely to have stretched across the mouth of the bay, with sand dunes and a brackish lagoon between it and the area of the present beach.[1] Coastal change presented just as much of a challenge to the Neolithic population of Orkney as it does to the population of today (Figure 16).

The coming of farming

It is almost inconceivable that we will ever find traces of the very first people to bring the new way of life to the islands; it would be akin to looking for a needle in a haystack. Moreover, it is also likely that the new ways were not well developed at first, thus making them difficult to recognise. Archaeology tends only to recognise change once it has become established. The periods of initial contact and slow assimilation of ideas that would have affected the people who lived here are hard to see.

What we do know is that by 3500 BC the basis of life in the islands had changed. The economic mainstay had shifted to the cultivation of crops and the husbandry of animals, but the changes were more far reaching than that. There were some innovations in material culture, including changes to the stone and bone tools and the introduction of pottery. Other changes led naturally from the new way of life: settlements became more permanent and substantial stone-built houses appeared; a new relationship with the land arose and this was celebrated with the construction of monuments to the ancestors. Archaeologically, this time is known as the Neolithic.

The people who were practicing this new way of life are likely to have been made up of the indigenous population, though some things must have been brought to the islands and this would have involved the arrival of some, if only a few, newcomers. Domesticated animals and seed, for example, must have been brought over by boat. Examples of the new-fangled pottery vessels and heavier stone tools such as axes are likely to have been packed beside them. Those who crewed the boats may well have shared different religious beliefs to the local population, and it would seem that their ideas were strong because the archaeological monuments soon show a quite distinct way of expressing their relationship with the world and the ancestors.

The first farmers

Perhaps the first boat groups to set out from mainland Scotland saw the islands across the Firth as fertile ground of which they could make use; it is likely that they needed new land. One of the side effects of the adoption of farming was that it provided a more reliable food-base, thus allowing the population to expand. While hunter-gatherers tend to conserve group size carefully so that they can feed everyone, farmers tend to need more and more hands to work the land. For a farming community it therefore becomes an advantage to have larger and larger families, but as each generation grows, so the community has to find new lands to occupy. Orkney must have offered just such a fertile new area (Figure 17).

Clearance was necessary to provide the space for crops and animals. We can but imagine how this would have seemed to the local hunters. Ironically, though their way of life had successfully supported them for many thousands of years, its collapse is likely to have been relatively quick. As the natural woodland was cleared, the wind could penetrate among the surviving trees, thus affecting further growth. Fields of crops and small herds of animals would have quickly provided competition for space with the existing wild game. Some of the Mesolithic foragers themselves would no doubt have been attracted to the new ways of life, though others may have been more resistant. The world of Mesolithic Orkney soon disappeared forever, to be replaced by the treeless landscape that is more familiar today.

New buildings, new beliefs

The first farmers settled into Orkney, making use of the local stone to build spacious farmsteads from which to work the land. Some lived in isolated settlements, others in small villages. Community life changed; there was time, and the need, to build monuments. Houses for the dead were built, similar to the tombs that were used for the ancestors in mainland Scotland. No doubt some of the old population stuck to old ways, disposing of the dead as they had always done (in a way that has left no archaeological trace), but others took on the new ideas and with time stone tombs became common. Other monuments were also important. Circular henge sites were built, within which settings of timber posts and standing stones were laid out for ceremonial purposes. The ritual aspects of life are unlikely to have been kept separate from domestic life in the way that we know today; many elements of the spiritual world would have permeated daily life and devotion could be undertaken at home or in the fields, as well as in those places set aside for it.

New goods

The innovations of the Neolithic are important for the archaeologists who study the remains of these times. The traces of the Neolithic population of Orkney are plentiful in comparison with those of Mesolithic Orkney. This is partly because more use was made of materials that do not degrade in the same way as those which characterise Mesolithic remains. Houses were built of stone, ceremonial centres of turf and stone, and pottery and new stone tools were used. Even the traces cut by the Neolithic ploughs have occasionally been found where they penetrated sandier sub-soils below the modern plough soil.

Neolithic pottery, in particular, has been well studied. It has been used to identify and sub-divide the Neolithic communities of Orkney and look at their relationship with the population of mainland Britain.[2] In common with the

people of today, those of the past were slaves to fashion and, although we do
not have their surviving clothes, it is possible to see changing fashions in other
accessories and everyday goods, including pottery. Different forms of pottery
have been interpreted in various ways, from pots that served different func-
tions to those that reflect different groups. The pottery of Neolithic Orkney
has been divided into two distinct traditions.[3] There is still some debate among
archaeologists as to the precise reasons for this,[4] but there are other changes in
material culture that roughly mirror those in pottery styles and together these
are generally interpreted as indicative of overlapping earlier (3800–3000 BC)
and later periods (3500–2500 BC) among the first farmers.[5]

Early Neolithic, Late Neolithic

The pottery from earlier times is known as Unstan Ware. These vessels
comprised fine shallow bowls with round bottoms, sometimes with incised
decoration. Later pottery had flat bottoms and deeper sides. The later pots
were often bucket shaped, and elaborately decorated with applied cordons,
bosses, and swags; they are known as Grooved Ware. Of course, we have no
idea how the people of Neolithic Orkney identified themselves, and pottery is
likely to have been only a part of the ways in which distinct groups were recognized. Unstan Ware sites are less common than Grooved Ware sites, and
Unstan Ware is relatively rare outside of Orkney. Grooved Ware, in contrast,
is well known right across Britain, though oddly it is most common in
two extremes: Orkney, in the north; and Wessex, in the south of England
(Figure 18).

   The interpretation that there were two phases to the Neolithic in Orkney is
mirrored across Scotland, and indeed Britain, though the quality of the
evidence from Orkney means that some of the best information comes from
these islands. The division is supported by the architectural evidence, both
from settlements and from tombs.

The dwellings of the first farmers

The settlements of Early Neolithic Orkney included isolated farmsteads. The
site at the Knap of Howar in Papa Westray was regarded for many years as
typical of Early Neolithic Orkney, and though other settlement types are
now known from the period, Knap of Howar is still one of the most famous
Early Neolithic sites, and well worth a visit. Knap of Howar is particularly
well preserved.[6] It comprises a low stone farmstead of two conjoining structures. Each provided a long, sub-divided, internal space with rounded ends.
The larger structure seems to have comprised the living quarters and was
divided into two roughly equal parts, within which traces of stone and timber
furnishings survive. The smaller structure seems to have been used more as a
workshop and was divided into three sections, also containing stone furnishings. The structures at Knap of Howar were sunk into a mound of midden

FIGURE 18.
A highly decorated
sherd of Grooved
Ware.

© THE TRUSTEES OF
THE NATIONAL
MUSEUMS OF
SCOTLAND

FIGURE 19.
This small vessel made
of whalebone comes
from Skara Brae and
gives a good impression
of the versatility of the
Neolithic craft workers.

© THE TRUSTEES OF
THE NATIONAL
MUSEUMS OF
SCOTLAND

FIGURE 20.
Excavation work by
Orkney Archaeological
Trust taking place at
Ness of Brodgar in
2004.

C. WICKHAM-JONES

material which provided stability to the stone buildings, as well as being an important method of insulation.

The finds from the Knap of Howar included stone and bone tools as well as pottery (Figure 19). The people who lived here were self-sufficient farmers, able to supply their needs from the land and resources around them. They are likely to have lived in a small extended family with unmarried uncles and aunts, as well as the elder generation all playing their part. The farmstead stands alone, though it is likely that other families lived not far away. The incorporation of midden as a structural element is intriguing because it indicates pre-existing settlement in the vicinity of Knap of Howar, though none has yet been found.

Indications of larger settlements of Early Neolithic date have also been found in Orkney, especially in recent years. Excavations at Ness of Brodgar (Figure 20), by the Ring of Brodgar, and at Pool in Sanday have revealed Neolithic structures that may include Early Neolithic buildings.[7] Other sites are more ambiguous, largely because excavation did not uncover a sufficiently wide area. Excavations at the later site of Howe, outside Stromness, revealed the possible remains of an Early Neolithic house, though it is difficult to set it into context. Stonehall and Wideford, both in the Finstown area, are other good examples. Both these sites yielded a substantial stone-built structure, of similar design and with similar goods to Knap of Howar, but it is not possible to be certain whether these farmsteads represent isolated examples. In addition, Wideford added another element to the Early Neolithic repertoire with the discovery of traces of two timber buildings, one rectangular and the other circular in plan. It is clear that the people of Early Neolithic Orkney lived in settlements of varying size, and used a variety of building materials.

Burial among the farmers

Tombs as well as houses differ in style between the the Early and Late Neolithic,[8] although there are, of course, tombs that cross the divide, emphasising the blurring of our modern classifications which had no meaning for those who lived at the time. In general, earlier tombs are known as Orkney-Cromarty cairns. They comprise an entrance passage leading to a central chamber that may be tripartite or divided by stone uprights into a series of stalls. Good examples of the Orkney–Cromarty cairns include Blackhammer and Midhowe in Rousay, both of which may be visited (Figure 21).

The site of Unstan, which gave its name to the style of pottery found there, is another Early Neolithic tomb, this time of a hybrid variety; though it is divided internally into stalls it also incorporates a small side cell that leads off the main chamber. Unstan lies on the shore at the south end of the Loch of Stenness, close to the World Heritage Sites.

In the past many tombs were found to contain large quantities of human bone, though our understanding of how they were used has been adversely affected by the fact that few survived intact for modern archaeology. Chambered tombs have always been prominent features of the landscape; this was probably a deliberate strategy on the part of their builders, but over the millennia it has left them vulnerable to exploration and robbing. Despite this, however, it does seem that not all tombs were used in quite the same way.[9] Some contained piles of disarticulated human bone; others had recognisably articulated skeletons. Some contained all the bones from a body; others had only a few bones, apparently representative of many individuals. In some cases bodies were apparently exposed prior to incorporation in the tomb; but other bodies were apparently laid in the tomb very soon after death. One common feature is that all tombs seem to have been designed to be entered repeatedly, perhaps even on occasions that did not involve a new burial. Communication with the spirit world, or some sort of relationship with those who were already there, seems to have been important.

These tombs represent quite different methods of burial to those that had gone before. The deposition of the dead in Mesolithic Scotland has left no archaeological trace, but elsewhere in Europe people were laid to rest in shallow graves. We are not sure whether all members of the Neolithic community were buried in the tombs, but it seems unlikely, though we have yet to find any remains relating to other types of burial. We can be sure, however, that the tombs mark a new relationship between the people, their ancestors, and the land. Permanence and the marking of place had become important and there is evidence from many tombs that ceremonies took place both outside and inside the main structure. In addition to the human bones many tombs contained artefacts such as stone tools and pot sherds, though whether these are grave goods or ceremonial relics from the living is uncertain. Animal bones were also incorporated and in some instances these have been interpreted as indicative of totemic spirits that were attached to the different communities.[10]

The development of ritual sites

It is more difficult to identify ceremonial sites from the Early Neolithic because many of them were used and remodelled over time, so that later remains sit on top of them. Nevertheless, this was the time when the foundations of the ceremonies and associated sites that we identify with the Neolithic were put in place. Activity seems to have started early at the Stones of Stenness, and there is a suggestion that the tomb of Bookan and an associated henge site at the other end of the Brodgar peninsula may also relate to the Early Neolithic.

Interestingly, the ritual needs that required the construction of large ceremonial monuments only developed once the farming communities were well settled. In this respect it is important to remember that the very act of building may have been an important part of the ceremony. Just as the construction of a cathedral had important things to say about the cohesion, wealth and aspirations of a community in medieval Europe, so the planning and layout of a henge, the raising of a standing stone, or filling of a pit, are likely to have had a special importance that is difficult to understand today.

The Early Neolithic in the World Heritage Area

In the World Heritage Area hard evidence of the Early Neolithic is lacking, though towards the end of this time the area of the Brodgar isthmus first became important in a way that has left physical archaeological traces. The foundations of the World Heritage Sites, though invisible today, were developing in the Early Neolithic.

The settlement at Barnhouse may have been founded towards the end of this time (Figure 22),[11] and new archaeological evidence suggests that there may have been early houses at Ness of Brodgar as well. Those who lived in these villages must have been familiar with developments at the Stones of Stenness, where the henge was under construction, and perhaps with work at Bookan too. Recent excavations have also uncovered indications of early structures beneath Maeshowe, though it is not possible to interpret these clearly.

FIGURE 21.
Interior of the tomb at Midhowe, Rousay. The long central chamber was divided into sections by upright stone slabs.
CHARLES TAIT

FIGURE 22.
House at Barnhouse by
the Stones of Stenness.

RAYMOND PARKS

To the west, the first houses at Skara Brae were being built and it is easy to imagine that the people there must have known, and perhaps participated in, the grand scale of the work that was going on between the lochs.

Local tombs from this time include Unstan, and possibly that at Bookan. It is almost impossible to associate the human remains from an individual tomb with a specific settlement site, but the proximity of these burial sites to settlements such as Barnhouse and the possible site at Ness of Brodgar is highly suggestive.

CHAPTER FOUR

Skara Brae:
Settling Down and Taming
the Land in the Late Neolithic

....

Introduction

By 3000 BC farming was well established as the way of life in Orkney, though the accumulated wisdom of the Mesolithic was still important. Fishing[1] and hunting[2] provided important supplements to the diet, and the use of other wild resources included the collection not just of foodstuffs such as berries and mushrooms, but of other useful plants such as puff balls and sphagnum moss.[3] At Skara Brae the midden deposits around the houses have provided unusual evidence of diet and other aspects of life that rarely survives on other sites. This has allowed the specialists to reconstruct the Neolithic lifestyle in unusual detail.[4]

The inhabitants of Orkney were settled in stone-built villages but they maintained contact with the outside world. Skara Brae was one such village, but there were many others, and dispersed farmsteads probably also existed alongside these.[5] The population of Orkney may not have been that different to today: some 20,000 people. The foundations of the great ceremonial sites across the Brodgar Peninsula were already well established, but it is at this time that they began to take on the architectural shape that has remained to this day.

Settlement remains

Many Stone Age villages are known across Orkney, but the first to be discovered, and perhaps still the best preserved and best known, is Skara Brae (Figure 23). That this should be so is ironic, since although the ruins were particularly visible, the true age of Skara Brae was a matter of some fierce debate for over 70 years. Initially many antiquarians thought that Skara Brae was Pictish (a little over 1,000 years old), and it was not until 1936 that Stuart Piggott suggested, on the basis of the pottery found there, that it might be Neolithic.[6] By the 1950s this was the accepted view,[7] though Skara Brae was not really placed into a broader context until the advent of widespread programmes of radiocarbon dating in the early 1970s.

Moreover, the very quantity of data available from the site has worked against it. There were two separate excavation projects at Skara Brae in the 1970s, each designed to answer very specific questions. The first took place within the settlement and related to the use of midden for house construction. The second was designed to look at the possibility of further archaeological remains outside the area cared for by Historic Scotland, but in the end it found only evidence for farming activity such as field dykes. The careful use of detailed excavation techniques meant that both of these projects resulted in the collection of a huge amount of data, analysis of which is only just nearing completion, some 30 years later. Skara Brae is a key site, but there is no doubt that the lack of published information on the 1970s excavations has been detrimental (Figure 24).

The physical remains of Skara Brae have been described earlier in this volume (pages 5–12) and there are many other publications which go into more detail. For many years archaeologists wondered whether Skara Brae was something special or set apart and this attitude is still reflected in some of their interpretations of the site. However, we now know that villages like this were common across Orkney. At least five similar village sites have been partially excavated and the remains of several others are known.

Construction work at Skara Brae

Those who built the houses at Skara Brae drew on specific and precise building skills. There was no shortage of good building stone in the vicinity of the site, and this was combined with sticky midden material that provided both insulation and stability. The basic shape of the houses was a practical one and the stone furnishings suggest the application of wisdom that had accumulated over several generations. The similarity of one house to another limited the need for specialist input, but some organisation of the process must have taken place.

It is possible that the earlier houses were freestanding, like those at Barnhouse, but by the later years of the settlement Skara Brae had become a much more cohesive entity that incorporated covered passages leading from one house to another (Figure 25). This must have eased life through the Orcadian winters. In common with any village community it is likely that construction was an on-going process as houses fell into disrepair or needed alteration.

Stone for the walls may have been abundant, but the roofing materials have presented more of a conundrum to modern archaeologists. The houses survive to roof level, but there is little indication of how they might once have been covered. Stone roofs, though common in historical times, are unlikely on the grounds of both weight and lack of evidence – if stone had been used some trace would surely have survived. Wood is a distinct possibility, even though the Orcadian woodland had, by then, largely disappeared. Driftwood timbers would have washed up on local shores, and many would have been substantial, including material from the northern shores of North America, in

FIGURE 23.
Interior detail of one of
the Skara Brae houses.
RAYMOND PARKS

addition to trees from the European forests. Frameworks of whalebone might also have been used for the roofs at Skara Brae, though no direct evidence for this has survived.

The covering of the roof's framework may well have been made of turf, though some roofs might have used skins. Some may have been thatched with straw, and rope of twisted heather or straw weighted with stones would have been vital to hold the roofing materials down (Figure 26). In the centre of the roof a lumb, or smoke-hole, may have let smoke out and some light in, though it is possible that the roof was without a direct exit for smoke – strange though

Skara Brae: Settling Down and Taming the Land in the Late Neolithic

FIGURE 24 (*left*). Excavation work taking place at Skara Brae in the 1970s.

CROWN COPYRIGHT, REPRODUCED COURTESY OF HISTORIC SCOTLAND AND THE TRUSTEES OF THE NATIONAL MUSEUMS OF SCOTLAND

FIGURE 25 (*right*). Covered passages wind between the houses at Skara Brae.

C. WICKHAM-JONES

this might seem, it worked well in Hebridean blackhouses where the smoke dispersed inside to act as a natural disinfectant, and the thatch provided a rich fertiliser when it was stripped off during maintenance each year.[8]

All in all, the people of Skara Brae knew how to build a home that would be both sheltered and stable. Their design has stood the test of centuries, giving us the remarkable remains of the present day.

Food for the body

The people of Skara Brae lived in families not unlike those of today. They were, in many ways, just like us, though without the trappings of modern life. It is likely that many homes included grandparents or other relatives and tasks were probably divided according to age and gender. Food came from the fields: they grew barley and wheat and kept cattle, sheep and pigs. In the light of accumulations of red deer bones at a few sites some archaeologists have suggested that red deer may also have been farmed,[9] though this is controversial.[10] In addition to meat, there was milk, and the products of hunting, fishing and gathering would also have been important to vary the diet. Between the village and the sea (which lay about a mile to the west of the village) lay a

FIGURE 26.
Rope made from
twisted heather, found
at Skara Brae. Heather
rope, known as
simmans, was common
in Orkney until recent
times and is still to be
found here.
CROWN COPYRIGHT,
REPRODUCED
COURTESY OF
HISTORIC SCOTLAND

brackish lagoon which was good for wild-fowling; there were also plentiful shellfish to be harvested on the shore and cod and saithe were caught, probably from the rocky coastline. Eggs could be harvested from the nearby cliffs. Inland, deer may have been hunted, and at certain times berries and mushrooms abounded. Much food would be eaten fresh, but some was dried and cured to last through the winter. Milk may well have been made into cheeses and fermented produce.

In contrast to the dietary habits of the early twenty-first century, the inhabitants of Skara Brae had to work hard to get fat into their diet, something that was especially important during the colder winter months. Milk was an obvious source, especially when turned into cheese, but much of their meat was still very lean, and fish and shellfish contain little fat. Other fatty foodstuffs included nuts, oily seabirds and marine mammals such as seals or whales. Whalebone artefacts were found at Skara Brae, and it is likely that the inhabitants made good use of any beached whales. Blubber is a rich source of vitamin C, another dietary essential through the winter months, and a single whale would supply plenty of blubber as well as bone for tools, among other things.[11] Smaller mammals such as seals could be killed relatively easily when they came ashore to pup in the late spring.

Light and heat

The houses were warm, but to us they would have seemed dark and smoky. There was not much ventilation. No obvious lamps have been found, but lighting would have been important though people did not, perhaps, need quite such well-lit interiors as we do today. Whale oil was one good source of lighting fuel, and oil could be extracted from other sea mammals and birds. Wicks were plentiful in the form of local rushes and small containers of stone, bone or pottery would all have served as reservoirs for the oil. When experimental lights are tried it often seems dark and dingy at first, but where people have made use of replica houses they quickly get used to lower levels of light. Of course some light would also come from the hearth and it is likely that the fire would be kept going round the clock. Fuel, however, could pose a problem, especially for a permanent settlement of several families. As the local woodland diminished, supplies of drift wood, burnable waste, seaweed and dried animal dung would have been used.

Heat was especially important in the winter when the outside temperature could drop to freezing and great storms of icy hail and wind might rage for days. It is likely that people went out as little as possible at that time, though there may have been stock to tend and from time to time the supplies of fuel would have needed replenishing. Clothing must have been efficient, though nothing tangible has survived to the present day. The lack of weaving equipment at Skara Brae suggests that clothing was made of hides and furs. There are plentiful needles and points among the bone tools that would have served to tailor them, as well as toggles and pins to be used as fastenings (Figure 27). In the winter, down from local wildfowl could be added for insulation. There are also beads and other trimmings, which suggest that some clothes were decorated, and ochre and haematite may well have been used along with other colouring materials such as charcoal to add variety.

Survival and multi-tasking in the Neolithic

Survival in the Neolithic was a matter of self-sufficiency. Life depended on how much food you had. The members of the Neolithic community trod a fine line between starvation and plenty in a way that has all but disappeared from twenty-first-century Britain, though it was part of life for many until relatively recently, particularly among rural communities, and it is still very much integral to the existence of many peoples around the world. The Neolithic inhabitants of Orkney had to grow enough food for everyone. If they did not, there was some nourishment to be collected from the wild resources that still abounded, but the rise in population generated by farming meant that bushcraft was no longer a sustainable way of life in the way that it had been for their Mesolithic ancestors some three thousand years earlier. If there was not enough food, then people would die.

This basic fact meant that the inhabitants of the community and the tasks of everyday life were inextricably bound into acts of ritual and religion. Over recent centuries, as we have come to take our everyday survival for granted, so we have come to separate religion from home, even to regard it as an optional 'add-on'. It was not so when life was more uncertain.

In order to be self-sufficient, the people of Skara Brae undertook a never-ending round of tasks that occupied both young and old. Education came on the hoof; the children learnt as they copied their elders and were given simple tasks to fulfil. In spring and summer there were fields to prepare, crops to sow

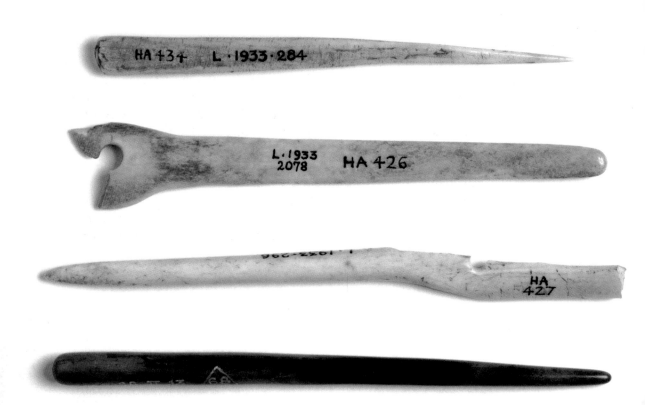

FIGURE 27.
Bone pins from Skara
Brae.

© THE TRUSTEES OF
THE NATIONAL
MUSEUMS OF
SCOTLAND

and animals to tend. Autumn brought a round of preparation for winter, food to lay in, fuel to collect, clothes to prepare and houses to make good. Even in winter there were tools to mend and replace, clothing to make, and animals to keep an eye on.

Tasks were no doubt divided according to age and ability, but individual survival meant that each member of the community had to be familiar with a wide range of skills. Tasks that we might regard as traditionally masculine or feminine were less clearly designated;[12] for example, it was vital for the hunters who ventured out in the colder weather to be able to repair their clothes and equipment. If they did not carry bone needles and sinew they would quickly succumb to the effects of exposure should their clothing snag on rocks or their ropes tear under pressure.[13] The stone artefacts suggest that most people had enough skill to make the everyday pieces that were a necessary part of the tool kit. They were also likely to have been competent potters, bone workers, and hide workers. Much of this could be done in the home, but some work was carried out elsewhere. House 8 at Skara Brae has a different internal arrangement which lacks the usual beds but includes many shelves and alcoves as well as enhanced facilities for heating. It is the only structure in the later part of the settlement to stand alone, and it seems to have been set aside for craftwork. If so, it is likely to have been used communally. A workshop such as this would be especially useful for making pots and flaking sharp stone tools, both of which required the specialist application of heat and, especially in the case of flint knapping, left debris that needed to be disposed of carefully (Figure 28).

Tasks at home were also linked to knowledge of the world away from the settlement. Stone tools, for example, required specific raw materials. The best stone with which to make a sharp blade or arrowhead is flint and this did occur naturally in prehistoric Orkney, though it was not abundant. Rounded pebbles of flint could be collected from the till deposits left behind by the glaciers as they crossed Orkney for the last time, and they also occurred in beach and river gravels as a result of erosion.[14] Most of the nodules were small, so that it was impossible to make anything big; any larger flint pebbles would have been carefully hoarded for the use of specialist knappers. Most of the prehistoric population across Orkney were able to collect enough flint for their needs but, interestingly, at Skara Brae many tools are made of an inferior stone, chert, that is available locally, and it seems as if flint was not as readily available in this area.[15]

FIGURE 28.
The workshop at Skara Brae.

RAYMOND PARKS

The emergence of specialist skills

In addition to the everyday skills of individual householders, there is evidence in Neolithic Scotland that some people had particular specialised skills and that the community was able to make use of them. This is an unusual step because it leads people away from the safety of self-sufficiency, but it is an important one. Some people, for example, were clearly skilled flint knappers, able to make artefacts such as finely flaked knives that would never be used in the home but rather incorporated into burials or used as a gift for the gods. Others made outsized pots, or enigmatic but highly carved stone balls and other strangely shaped stone objects. No doubt the time that was invested in producing these goods was repaid with food or other commodities such as clothing. Gradually the basis of life started to shift towards a very different economy in which people began to develop particular skills in exclusion to others (Figure 29).

Leisure

Life in Neolithic Orkney was not just about work. There was time to make jewellery and the opportunity to wear it. Other finds from the village look remarkably like dice and may well have been used for gaming, as may finds of cow knuckle bones.

Around Skara Brae there are incised markings which have been interpreted

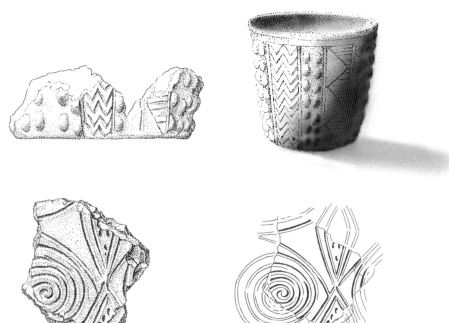

FIGURE 29.
Some of the pottery from Skara Brae was highly decorated. This reconstruction by Alexandra Shepherd shows how some of the original sherds may have looked (above), while (below) the elaborate decoration on this sherd is still a powerful motif today (see Figure 18).

as art (Figure 30).[16] Many of these occur on the stone slabs of the passage walls, but there are also some in the houses. The designs are all very abstract; lozenges and criss-cross lines predominate. There are also decorated artefacts, notably the Grooved Ware pottery but also bone pins and pendants as well as the occasional stone knife.[17] On most of these the same types of motifs appear. Art like this occurs on other Neolithic settlement sites, as at the villages of Barnhouse and Pool, and it is also found in other settings, especially those related to burial. At Maeshowe a series of triangles and diamond shapes have been scratched onto one of the great uprights by the entrance, and a cist slab from Brodgar has a series of incised bands with lozenge designs.

There have been many discussions relating to the interpretation of these scratchings, from representations of landscape to designs copied from the natural fracture of the local rocks.[18] Angular motifs like these contrast greatly with other Neolithic designs which incorporate softer, circular swirls and were more deeply pecked to produce strong visible patterns. At Pierowall in Westray the excavation of a chambered tomb revealed a great slab on which elaborate swirls and circles had been carefully incised, and there are other examples from

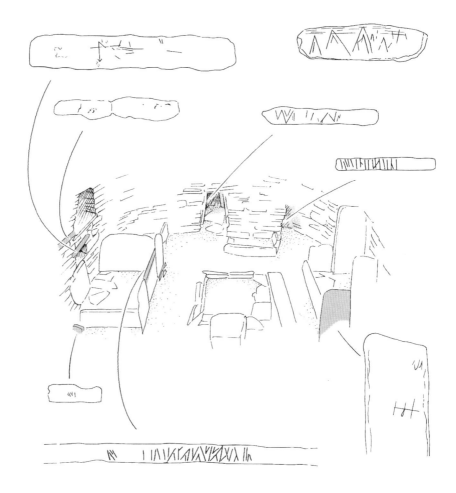

FIGURE 30.
Some of the art from Skara Brae. Alexandra Shepherd has been studying the art and its locations, and in this drawing she looks at some of the most popular motifs and their location within one of the houses.

Neolithic sites elsewhere, such as in the Boyne valley in Ireland and the passage tombs in Brittany.

Although we see art like this in monochrome, it was not necessarily so in the past. Arlene Isbister has been working with haematite, and she suggests that many of the small haematite finds from Skara Brae served as 'pencils' and colour sticks.[19] If haematite is wetted and rubbed on to a rough surface it yields a pigment that can either be applied directly or mixed with other things. Little pots of ochre pigment were found at Skara Brae, and there were, of course, many other substances from which colour could be produced in the Neolithic. Nature supplied a variety of plants, minerals and even shellfish which would yield various colours and it is likely that many were exploited. It is possible, therefore, that the simple incised lines that we see were once highlighted with colour, just as there may have been coloured swirls on the standing stones. Other pieces of art may have involved the decoration of hides, bodies, or wood, but all have of course been lost because of the decay of organic material.

Various elements of leisure also remain obscure. Music, rhythm and dance, for instance, are likely to have been important, but have left little trace. As we all know even the most mundane of household artefacts can be used to make rhythm, but there is no clear evidence for specific drums. Perforated bones have been interpreted as whistles, but these seem to have been used for dogs rather than aimed at the human ear.[20] Research on the acoustic properties of

FIGURE 31.
Skara Brae: one of the earlier houses lies in the foreground.
RAYMOND PARKS

various sites is just beginning[21] and we can only hope that in future some of these gaps in our understanding of life in the Neolithic will be filled.

When all was not well: illness in the Neolithic

In comparison to today, life at Skara Brae was hard, and this is reflected in elements such as life expectancy. Apart from the two burials in house 7 there are few human bones from Skara Brae, but we know from remains in tombs of the time, such as Isbister in South Ronaldsay, that few people lived to much over 40.[22] For women childbirth is likely to have been a major danger, but an unreliable diet, harsh life and the lack of effective medicines took their toll on all.[23] Children were especially vulnerable and those women who survived childbirth are likely to have outlived many of their children. For men there were other dangers, associated with their different tasks. Aggression too was not unknown. Although we have no direct evidence of aggression from Skara Brae, Neolithic burials from elsewhere show a wide range of injuries relating to violence, from arrow wounds to blows and breakages.

The community at Skara Brae is unlikely to have been powerless in the face of illness and injury, however. Many of the plants around them had special properties and it is probable that they knew and made use of these. Support for this is supplied by the finds of many small puff balls among the archaeological remains. Puff balls act as a blood clotting agent and were used in the past to dress wounds. The quantity of puff balls at Skara Brae suggests that they were collected for a specific purpose and this may well have involved their medicinal properties. Another local plant that would have been useful is sphagnum moss, which contains a natural antiseptic, though sphagnum is unlikely to survive on archaeological sites and to date none has been found on the sites of Neolithic Orkney. Evidence is emerging elsewhere for the use at this time of techniques that we still regard as alternatives to conventional medicine. Acupuncture, for example, has been recorded in relation to 'Ötzi the Iceman'.[24]

The world beyond: belief and ritual

Those who lived to be over 40 had a wealth of experience to pass on to others

FIGURE 32.
The largest building at Barnhouse is interpreted as having been used for ceremony.

RAYMOND PARKS

and this was no doubt reflected in their tasks and lifestyle. We know nothing of leadership in the community, though the lack of a 'big house' suggests that influence may well have been communal. Some aspects of life must have involved considerable organisation, as, for example, participation in the building of the communal henge monuments, though we know nothing of how this was arranged. It is possible that events such as these were organised outside of the community by those who held religious power, though there is as yet no clear evidence for a separate body of 'priests'.

Our understanding of Neolithic religion, like its art, remains unclear. Religion clearly existed, and would have been much more a part of everyday life than for most of us today. The distinctions that we make between 'religion' and 'life' are likely to have been meaningless in the Neolithic.[25] Ordinary homes, such as those at Skara Brae, must have provided the setting within which many religious acts took place. There were also, however, the great communal sites which were somehow set apart. The trip to the Brodgar Peninsula would not have been a long one; for the people of Skara Brae it would have been quite possible to travel there and back on foot in a day and still have time to participate in, or observe, the ceremonial. Those from further afield in Orkney would have to rely on water transport to reach the central heartland, and are likely to have spent at least a night there (something that has left, so far, no archaeological evidence, although there has been no targeted research in this matter). Elsewhere across Orkney there were many smaller locations, such as single standing stones, which must have served as the foci for local ceremonies, and we should not forget that unmarked natural places may also still have held a special significance.

All of these sites are likely to have been used for worship, though we do not know whether this was something in which the whole community – or only a few people – participated. It is possible that levels of participation varied according to the time of year and the age of the participants. It is also likely, however, that religion was directed in some way by those who had particular skills: those who could consult easily with the ancestors, communicate and interpret the spirit world, or just organise and direct the community. We do not know on what basis people became spiritual leaders and guides but the sophistication of the ceremonial and burial monuments suggests that they provided an effective force in society.

Everyday life in the World Heritage Area

Skara Brae may comprise the best-known settlement remains in the World Heritage Area but it is not alone. Even in this small area there are several Neolithic sites. After Skara Brae, the best known site is that of Barnhouse, beside the Standing Stones of Stenness, which was excavated in the 1980s by a team under the leadership of Colin Richards and which has recently been comprehensively published.[26]

The houses at Barnhouse comprised a group of at least 13 free-standing structures. As well as apparently domestic structures, the settlement included buildings that do not seem to have been designed as dwellings. Barnhouse dates to around 3200–3000 BC and most of the houses have sub-circular interiors with central hearths, drains and beds that were recessed into the walls. One of the less familiar building types comprises a large double-roomed structure with deep angled bays. There is also a large rounded building surrounded by a massive outer wall through which a monumental entrance provided access into a space that seems to have been designed for ritual and communal activities (Figure 32). The structures at Barnhouse are significant because they show important parallels with the earlier houses at Skara Brae.

The remains at Barnhouse were removed for study as part of the excavation process, but they have been rebuilt and consolidated by Orkney Islands Council so that Barnhouse is now an interesting site to visit. Despite the close relationship which must have existed between the people who lived in the houses at Barnhouse and the nearby monument at the Stones of Stenness, Barnhouse is not itself a World Heritage Site, largely because as we see it today it is a recreation of the original remains; it is, however, still an integral part of the World Heritage story.

Barnhouse was in use for less time than the settlement at Skara Brae. By 2600 BC settlement had ended, though it looks as if the largest building may have been built and used after the abandonment of the rest of the houses. This structure is quite different to the earlier houses, however, and its use seems to have combined elements of ceremony with those of domestic life.

Other settlement remains have been recovered in the World Heritage Area in the fields to the south of the Ring of Brodgar, now known as Ness of Brodgar. In 2003 a stone building very similar to structure 2 at Barnhouse was uncovered here, and further work in 2004 and 2005 confirmed the existence of a complex of remains that probably includes activity in both the Early and the Late Neolithic. The evidence at Ness of Brodgar does not just include settlement remains; there is material relating to early cultivation, massive stone walling, and an indication, from the geophysics, of a possible chambered tomb. Further work at Ness of Brodgar is clearly a priority for a better understanding of Neolithic activity in the vicinity of the ceremonial sites.

Elsewhere in the World Heritage Area, concentrations of Neolithic artefacts discovered in the ploughsoil in the early twentieth century suggest other settlement remains. One of the biggest concentrations lies around the sites at Bookan at the northern end of the peninsula. A variety of flint tools, as well as other material characteristic of the Late Neolithic, has been recovered here. At Skara Brae itself the use of decomposed midden in the construction of the houses indicates that other settlement remains lie close by. They may have disappeared into the sea, but it is clear that despite the wealth of information we already have concerning the World Heritage Area, there is plenty of scope for future archaeology.

CHAPTER FIVE

Maeshowe: Death, Burial and the Other World in the Late Neolithic

Death

Death represents a gateway between this world and the next. As such its interpretation is an integral part of religion, and has been well studied by scholars from many fields. The number of Neolithic tombs in Orkney, and the quality of their remains, have provided plentiful data relating to the people who lived in settlements such as Skara Brae, though, not surprisingly, this evidence can

FIGURE 33.
Aerial view of
Maeshowe.

JOHN LEITH

FIGURE 34.
Interior view of
Maeshowe.

CHARLES TAIT

be hard to understand. New information and new interpretations are put forward every year.

Maeshowe

Among the World Heritage Sites death is most clearly represented by the great tomb of Maeshowe, on the mainland at the south-eastern end of the Brodgar Peninsula. The first recorded entry of Maeshowe was made by James Farrer in 1861. He found the chamber full of earth and stones, and sadly almost empty of finds; he recovered a single fragment of human skull and some horse bones from under the rubble. There is thus a lot to be learned from the architecture and design of Maeshowe, but information relating to its original fill is lacking. This has to be supplied by analogy with tombs elsewhere (Figure 33).

Maeshowe is the largest of the Orkney tombs and epitomizes the chambered tombs of the Later Neolithic in the archipelago. There are a number of

Maeshowe-type tombs known in Orkney, each with side cells that lead off the central chamber. In contrast to the tombs of the Early Neolithic, this type of tomb is not known from mainland Scotland.

The building of Maeshowe

Work at Maeshowe started around 3000 BC. It is difficult to isolate the first activity here, although recent work by Colin Richards and others has uncovered evidence for structural remains below the tomb here, though the interpretation of these is still speculative.[1] Remains of a stone-built drain that apparently pre-dates construction of the tomb may indicate that the earliest structure here comprised a dwelling or ceremonial building. We do not know for how long this building stood, but at some point it was deliberately levelled or left ruinous, for it was then covered with clay. At this point the circular platform that we see today took shape. The clay was used to create a level surface, the deep ditch was excavated, and an external bank was raised. Richards' work suggests that the bank may have been faced with stone. Maeshowe at this point was already an impressive monument, with obvious similarities in design to the henge sites (see Chapter Six). This provides the setting for the later elements of the monument. If Maeshowe did start life as a ceremonial centre, then it is interesting that the focus of activity later shifted geographically about one kilometre to the north-west, to the narrow stretch of land between the lochs.

The next activity at Maeshowe seems to have involved the four great stones which now stand at the corners of the central chamber. It has been suggested that they originally stood as an open air setting[2] and in his recent work Richards has pointed out that they do not, indeed cannot, form an integral part of the tomb structure because they would destabilize it. It is thus most likely that they were originally erected as free-standing standing stones on the platform at the heart of the monument. We do not know how long they stood apart, but they may have been used to help with the precise alignment of the passageway into the tomb, and with time as the tomb itself rose up they were incorporated into the chamber at its heart. The passage took shape, the chamber and side cells were carefully laid out towards the solstice, and slabs of flagstone were laid in place to form the cells and corbelled roof. Reinforcement may have been necessary behind the great corner slabs at this point, as they would tend to destabilize the structure. These stone uprights were obviously regarded as vital to the success of the tomb, so that it was worth overcoming the physical problems that they posed (Figure 34).

Immediately covering the chamber the builders laid an inner stone core to provide some protection. The mound on top of this is constructed of clay and stones and rises to a height of seven metres. Today the exterior of the mound is covered in turf, though at other sites alternative, and more impressive, exterior materials have been suggested. Newgrange, in Ireland, is perhaps the most notable; here a steep exterior façade of sparkling white quartz has been reconstructed. There is no evidence for quartz at Maeshowe, but the soft green turf that we see today may be misleading.

A further complication in the story of Maeshowe is represented by the discovery, in 1991, of a stone socket that once held a standing stone, on the platform to the rear of the mound. This is difficult to interpret. It may have formed part of a pre-existing stone circle here, for though geophysical survey has revealed little evidence of other stone sockets, they could be masked by the clay capping later spread to level the platform. On the other hand, the erection of this standing stone may have taken place later than the tomb. Excavations at a passage grave at Howe, not far from Maeshowe, have also revealed a standing stone which seems to have been erected after the tomb.[3]

The building of Maeshowe required considerable effort. It has been suggested that over 100,000 man-hours would have been necessary. It seems likely that work such as this would have involved many different communities and it may well be that people travelled across Orkney to participate. Stone working is likely to have taken place on site, because the internal slabs in the ceiling have been carefully dressed to provide a smooth appearance. Maeshowe represents a feat of organisation requiring careful planning not only for the building work, but also to provide food and shelter for the workforce. It is likely that there was some sort of centralised direction, perhaps from the spiritual leaders who would later control the use of the tomb. The attention to detail, even in places that would not be on view to all, emphasises the importance of the building. Other, external, details are equally impressive and must have been carefully thought out. The sheer scale of Maeshowe sets it apart from the other monuments of Neolithic Orkney, and Richards has suggested that the ditch may have been water-filled, thus emphasising the other-worldliness, or apartness, of the monument.

Treatment of the dead

Despite the lack of precise evidence, it is likely that once it was built Maeshowe was soon used as a burial place. Perhaps the initial occupant had already died prior to the initiation of building work. If so then an important element of Neolithic burial ritual must have come into play, that of the treatment of the dead between death and final burial.

The exposure of bodies on open platforms prior to incorporation in a tomb – excarnation – continued into the Late Neolithic.[4] This suggests a very different attitude to the dead and their remains from that of the modern era. Today we are keen to remove the dead from the sight and realm of the living as soon as possible. In the Neolithic it seems that people did not shrink from handling the remains of the dead, even some time after death. As the flesh was removed by a combination of carrion and decay, qualities of the personality may well have persisted in the bones. The skeleton became a vibrant element of the community, assisted, no doubt, by strong folk memory. Care was taken in some tombs to lay out the dead in skeletal form, but clearly this was not

always important because other tombs contain literally piles of bones which often mix one individual with another.

FIGURE 35.
The tomb at Wideford Hill.

CHARLES TAIT

Tombs for the living

The tombs were built to be entered and re-entered time and time again and this is a strong reminder that they were also places for the living. We do not

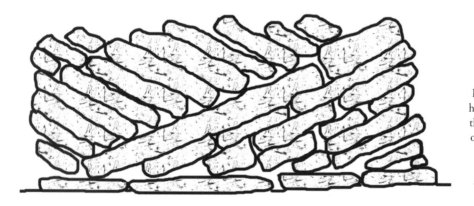

FIGURE 36.
Diagram to show the herringbone pattern in the exterior stonework of many of the tombs in Rousay:
Blackhammer stonework drawn by Sigurd Towrie.

60

know whether all members of a community could enter a tomb, but the evidence suggests not. Entrance is often difficult; the passages forced people to stoop low, a significant posture that surely tells us something of their relationship with the spirit world. The tomb interiors were not large and most would have held only a few people. Several of the tombs, including Maeshowe, had carefully made blocking stones at the entrance. At Maeshowe the blocking stone could be set in place from the inside, suggesting that it was important for those inside to restrict access and knowledge of what went on from the world outside. In addition, some tombs have sound boxes designed to convey noise, or communication, between the interior and the exterior. Others have gaps in the entrance stonework that may have served the same purpose.

The interior of a tomb was clearly the site of important activities that may well have incorporated more than the mere burial of the dead. With this in mind John Barber has suggested that the tombs were initially constructed as centres of worship and that the burials only came later, much as with Christian churches.[5] He draws information from the exterior of the tombs to suggest that they were carefully designed to impress. There is no denying, for example, the majesty of Maeshowe, even after five millennia of weathering and erosion. Other tombs may have had stepped exteriors; some were decorated. On Rousay many of the tombs have an elaborate herringbone pattern visible in the external stonework (Figure 36).

Most of the better-preserved tombs have specific spaces outside that seem to have been designed or set aside with activity in mind. Some, like Isbister in South Ronaldsay, have curved fronts that enhance their natural setting to create an amphitheatre shape. Many were sited to take advantage of impressive settings and backdrops. Maeshowe has the broad platform that encircles the tomb and is clearly set aside from the surrounding countryside by its ditch and bank. Where they have been excavated, the archaeological evidence from these spaces suggests that they were used for ceremony and ritual. They would clearly accommodate larger groups than might gain access to the interior of a tomb and they may thus have acted as important areas of mediation for the wider community. Barber's suggestion is that the tombs should be regarded more as temples.

This may seem far-fetched, but one thing we have learnt about human behaviour over the millennia is that far-fetched is often a good explanation! Whatever the precise activities that went on in and around the tombs, they highlight the importance of religion in a very tangible way.

The place of the ancestors

In general, the Neolithic tombs of Orkney suggest that the ancestors were particularly venerated, and that this was tied to a strong sense of place. Various studies have looked at the geographical spread of tombs. It is not (yet) possible to tie any one tomb to a particular community but the distribution of tombs suggests very strongly that they may have represented strong relationships with specific areas of land.

Home grounds are important to any human society, whether it is based on hunting or farming, but this relationship was enhanced with the advent of farming. The cultivation of fields and tending of stock restricted the daily range for most in the community and, for the first time, people not only lived in the same place all year round, but they could live there from one generation to the next. At the same time the well-being of the community was directly related to the well-being of its lands. In contrast to today, in the Neolithic this well-being was not something that humans could direct. Rather, it was considered to be in the hands of the world itself, or rather of the spirits and gods who made up the world. One way in which to propitiate them was to accord them careful rituals and offerings; another way was through the dead. The ancestors not only validated the presence of the community on the land, they could help to ensure its future. Impressive tombs could act both to venerate the ancestors and the world spirits, and as a marker that validated the link between a community and its lands.

The cist at Sand Fiold

If all members of a community were not buried in a tomb, then where were the rest? So far there has been little indication of Neolithic burial rites that did not involve interment in a chambered tomb. One hint came in 1989 with the discovery and excavation of a large stone-built cist in sand dunes not far from Skara Brae.[6] The slabs of the cist had been ingeniously put together so that it was possible to open one of the sides and re-enter the tomb. The contents of Sand Fiold cist were well preserved and they included both cremated bones and inhumated bones as well as pottery and the remains of basketry and mats. Normally this type of burial would have been considered to be Bronze Age, but Sand Fiold was unusual in its size, design and the complexity of the remains and so it was not surprising to find that it had been used over a long period that started in the Neolithic, sometime around 2800 BC. The earliest recorded use of the tomb at Sand Fiold comprised the burial of a new-born baby together with the ash from a cremation pyre. At least one other inhumation was later made in the tomb, and a pot containing cremated bone was placed inside; use of the tomb continued over some 900 years. Towards the end of its period of use there was some refurbishment of the cist and through time people appear to have cared for the contents.

The inhumation of bones and the designing of a tomb to allow it to be re-entered are well-known elements of the Neolithic burial tradition. Sand Fiold is unusual, but not, perhaps, unique. Records survive of a similar cist discovered in 1915 at Tormiston Farm close to Maeshowe, and in his publication of the Sand Fiold cist Magnar Dalland has suggested that use of the cist at Tormiston Farm may also have started in the Neolithic.

Maeshowe: Death,
Burial and the
Other World in the
Late Neolithic

Other types of treatment

The cists at Sand Fiold and Tormiston Farm provide an important indication of a possible Late Neolithic burial rite that did not involve chambered tombs, but to date the paucity of sites like them means that they are unconvincing as evidence for the burial rites of the majority of the population. Other hints may come from the complex settings at the heart of henges such as the Stones of Stenness. These include timber and stone features, as well as hearths, and they may well have been designed to include activities such as the treatment or disposal of the dead. It is impossible to be sure exactly how they were used, and settings such as this may well have been used for different things at different times of the year, or as need dictated.

It is quite possible that the majority of the dead were not 'buried' at all. Evidence of excarnation has, for example, been inferred from skeletal assemblages such as that at the Tomb of the Eagles, Isbister, in South Ronaldsay,[7] while elsewhere in Scotland excarnation platforms dating to the Neolithic have been excavated.[8] Bones may have been scattered or burnt after excarnation. Perhaps the sea was used: burial at sea is common in many societies and would normally leave no archaeological trace.

In this respect it is also important to remember that burial in Mesolithic Scotland has, so far, left no trace discernable today. Changes to belief and ritual are complex processes and it is quite possible that an element of Mesolithic tradition persisted into the Neolithic to influence burial practice for the majority of the ordinary population. It is salutary to remember the two skeletons found in the upper layers of House 7 at Skara Brae; had they been buried elsewhere, in less favourable preservation conditions, there would have been little hint of their presence today. Do they represent the type of burial accorded to the majority of the population of Neolithic Orkney?

The Maeshowe effect

Among the World Heritage Sites burial is represented by Maeshowe, but as we have seen, the remains of Neolithic burial were lacking in this tomb. Quite apart from its achievement and grandeur, Maeshowe does, however, shed light on another important aspect of Neolithic ritual. The entrance passage at Maeshowe was carefully built to line up with the setting sun of the midwinter solstice. Today the sun shines down the passage to light up the rear wall of the chamber and the entrance to the back cell for a few days on either side of the solstice and in the past, even with the shifts in the axis of the earth through time, the effect would have been similar (Figure 37).[9]

The alignment of Maeshowe also has an additional effect. The Neolithic design is such that when the blocking stone is in place across the entrance of the passage there is a horizontal slit above the stone through which the sun can penetrate to light up the inner chamber. Similar features are seen at other Neolithic tombs, perhaps the most famous being that of Newgrange in

FIGURE 37.
The Maeshowe effect:
the sun shining
through the entrance
passage of Maeshowe at
the midwinter solstice.
CHARLES TAIT

Ireland. Today a webcam captures the Maeshowe solstice and broadcasts it on the Internet for viewers around the world (www.maeshowe.co.uk). It may seem magical to us but the experience must have been breathtaking for the privileged few in the Neolithic who could enter and view it.

We perhaps draw nearer to our Neolithic ancestors when we realise that the designers of Maeshowe were able to do more than just incorporate this effect into their conception of the tomb. They also built in a safety margin to guard against the uncertainties of Orkney weather. The Maeshowe effect takes place for several days either side of the solstice. As it is by no means certain that the sun will appear on 21 December, this is a practical precaution.

We can experience the magic of the Maeshowe effect today, but we do not know its full meaning for those who experienced it 5,000 years ago. It is, however, another important indication of the value of the tombs as places of ritual as well as burial. This aspect of ritual becomes even more relevant when we look at the use of the henge sites and stone circles. The passage of time, the marking of the seasons, and the reappearance of the sun were all of crucial importance to a society that relied on cultivation and the fertility of the land for its sustenance. The entrance of the sun into the chamber at Maeshowe at

FIGURE 38.
Burial mounds cluster
around the Ring of
Brodgar, visible here on
the sky-line behind the
stones.
SIGURD TOWRIE

the precise moment when its journey through the sky was weakest is surely highly significant.

Burial in the World Heritage Area

Despite the pre-eminence of Maeshowe, there are other burial remains in the World Heritage Area.[10] At the northern end of the peninsula lie the remains of the chambered tomb of Bookan. This was explored in the nineteenth century by George Petrie, a local antiquarian. It seems to have been designed as a hybrid-type tomb with both side cells and central slabs to divide the chamber. This would suggest that Bookan was early, though the pottery found by Petrie suggests a Late Neolithic date. In addition to pot sherds and some flint, Petrie found human bone in three of the cells. Further excavations took place at Bookan in 2002, under the leadership of Nick Card.[11] These emphasised the ways in which the structure had continued to be developed as an impressive building, even after the original tomb had gone out of use. They seem to add weight to John Barber's suggestion that burial was only one of the ceremonial activities that took place at the tombs.

Close by the tomb of Bookan lie the dilapidated remains of the Ring of Bookan. This site has not been excavated in modern times, but it is generally regarded as the remains of a ceremonial henge site, though local stories tell of a central chamber that could be explored in previous centuries. On these grounds, it also was once considered to be a chambered tomb, though this theory has recently fallen out of favour.

The Ring of Brodgar is surrounded by burial mounds, most of which relate to the Bronze Age when it was clearly fashionable, or desirable, to be laid to rest in the vicinity of the great ceremonial site (Figure 38). One of the mounds, Salt Knowe, to the west of the Ring of Brodgar, has been suggested as a Neolithic chambered tomb on the grounds of its great size, though there is no hard evidence for this. The recent discovery of geophysical traces, highly suggestive of a chambered tomb, on the lower ground to the south-east of the Ring of Brodgar, where the peninsula narrows, shows just how much there is still to be learnt.[12] Further afield, on the southern edge of the World Heritage Area, lies Tormiston Farm, where the cist burial mentioned above was discovered. And to the south-west, opposite the Standing Stones Hotel in Stenness, rises a substantial mound. This was long presumed to be natural, but recent geophysical work suggests that it may be a chambered tomb and this is supported by nineteenth-century references.

It is possible that burial is a more important element of the World Heritage Area than is currently recognised. Much of the evidence for tombs is circumstantial, and the emphasis on known archaeological sites, in this case Maeshowe, has led to its being somewhat underplayed. The trend in archaeology in the twenty-first century is to look at landscapes rather than individual sites and in this way the evidence from other, less well-preserved, sites comes into its own.

Maeshowe: Death,
Burial and the
Other World in the
Late Neolithic

Maeshowe itself is, however, likely to have been special. It supports the current theories relating to burial and tomb use in the Neolithic, but in an exaggerated way. It has always been a dominating structure. There is no evidence as to how it was perceived into the Bronze Age, but it is likely to have gone out of use with the changes in ceremony, and presumably belief, that came about at that time. There is no evidence at Maeshowe for the small secondary cist burials that were sometimes inserted into the make-up of earlier tombs elsewhere. That in itself is perhaps evidence of the esteem in which Maeshowe has always been held. Not until the time of the Norse, some 4,000 years later, does Maeshowe once again enter the picture as an active site, and that period in its history is considered below (Chapter Nine).

CHAPTER SIX

The Brodgar Peninsula:
Dances of Stones

....

The people of Neolithic Orkney built great ceremonial sites in which to proclaim their beliefs and practice their ceremonies; some of these sites have survived to the present day. The Ring of Brodgar and the Stones of Stenness were but part of a great ceremonial landscape that occupied the whole of the Brodgar peninsula. Burial is just one aspect of the wider spiritual world which was designed (if not consciously) by and for the living, and another physical manifestation of this world lies in these ceremonial monuments.

The animate world

The Neolithic inhabitants of Orkney occupied a world that was different to our world of today in many ways. Quite apart from the lack of modern arte-facts, they saw their world as much more animate than we do. The world of the twenty-first century European (my world) is sharply divided in two, between sentient beings – people, and animals, fish and birds – and inanimate beings – rocks, fence posts, cars, houses, and so on. The place of trees and other plants in our order of things depends on where you stand along this environmental scale of sentience: do you, for example, talk to your plants?

Life was not as simple in the past. It is probable that the Skara Brae villagers not only talked to the trees but that they also respected the spiritual beings of stones, streams and vegetation. People may well have communicated with rocks (Figure 39). In the world of Neolithic Orkney, humans were but one part of an active environment in which nothing happened by chance. Wind and rain, moonlight and stars, warmth and cold, all represented deliberate actions on the part of the spirits or gods. The standing stones may well have held individual characteristics, just as trees and crops were propitiated before harvesting, or thanks were given for the spirit of an animal that was about to give its life to provide food and raw materials.

We do not, of course, know the names by which the spirit world was invoked, nor do we know the precise beliefs by which people made sense of the way their world worked. Our world outlook is so different that it can be difficult to imagine how things were for the prehistoric people of Orkney. It is hard to see the stone strainer in the corner of a field as watching over us (though many of us ascribe personalities to our cars, particularly when they do not behave as we would wish). Archaeology has provided us with physical evidence for the actions of the past. This ranges from the great circles of standing stones to handfuls of broken pots and we have to work from this evidence to construct an idea of what sort of beliefs existed and how they were carried out.

There are other features that can help us in our quest to understand the world belief of Neolithic Orkney. Hints of a very different system of beliefs survive in local stories and traditions. We do not know how far back stories of dancing standing stones or trows (supernatural beings, 'ugly, stunted little creatures, considerably smaller than a man'[1]) inside chambered tombs may reach,[2] but they provide a clear sign that all has not always been as we know it. Elsewhere in Europe people left offerings besides springs, or carved names to transfer the souls of the dead into living trees well into the nineteenth century. A belief in a living world is not confined to the Northern Isles; it was once widespread, though of course it has been manifest in many different ways. Ethnographic evidence thus supplies another important strand of information.

However clearly we think we see into the other world that comprised Neolithic Orkney, it is also important to remember that our ideas are just interpretation. We cannot know precisely what people believed or did, but we can make a good guess at how they saw things. We can write a story.[3] This story may be written in quite a different way in ten years' time, but it is a good story nonetheless.

FIGURE 39.
Some of the stones of
the Ring of Brodgar.
RAYMOND PARKS

Holy leaders

Ceremonies such as the ones that took place at the Ring of Brodgar were designed by the living as a manifestation of their beliefs. They might have been aimed at pleasing, or communicating with the gods, but they also served to hold together the community. In Neolithic Orkney, the sophistication and complexity of many of the monuments suggests that a variety of complex ceremonies took place. This in itself suggests an organised system, both of actual beliefs and of ritual. It is likely that this system was managed and upheld by particular people. They may have been elders, 'wise men', or 'earth mothers': perhaps the easiest term for us to use is 'priest'. The existence of priests is supported by the evidence from the chambered tombs which were designed to allow repeated, but restricted access. It seems that only a handful of people at any one time could make use of the setting inside a chambered tomb.

The presence of priests as a group within society is interesting because it is another tentative manifestation of specialists in the community. It may be that the priests also played a full role in everyday life. They may have worked to till the land and tend their animals as well as directing the spiritual well-being of the world. It seems, though, more likely that spiritual work took both time and effort, so that in many aspects of day-to-day life the priests were supported by the rest of the group. We do not know if they lived apart. Skara Brae has been interpreted as a religious community, and though that argument is not supported here for reasons explained above (Chapter One), Richards has suggested that there may have been differences in use between the structures.[4] At Barnhouse, one larger house, house 2, has six big recesses that have been interpreted as bed spaces.[5] House 2 is quite different to the other structures at Barnhouse and it remained in use for longer, while the other houses went in and out of use (Figure 40). Perhaps it provided priestly accommodation? The uniformity of Neolithic settlement across Orkney suggests that there were no specialised communities, or that if there were they have yet to be found.

Building the sites

Further support for the existence of a class of priests comes from the physical presence of the ceremonial sites themselves. Just laying out the site, amassing the stone and building the monument all required considerable, and well organised, effort. The basic layout must have been set out by a knowledgeable few, and it is likely that they continued to organise a workforce, even after the design was agreed. We do not know whether the monuments went up over a short space of time or whether they took longer to build, but current thinking suggests that they may have evolved slowly and that the act of building may well have been as important as the finished site. This is likely to have been a massive communal effort that may well have involved communities from across Orkney. Repeated visits may have taken place over the decades. The logistics were immense. Most groups would have needed overnight shelter, quantities of food would have to be prepared and (more importantly from the archaeologists' point of view) there would be waste to be disposed of. So far, however, no archaeological trace from the process of building has been found.

We can suggest the actual work that must have been involved. For the henges there was the ground to prepare, a circle to lay out, the ditch to dig, and upcast to stabilise into a bank. Once this was done internal activities could take place, and these no doubt involved the construction of hearths, post settings and even structures. It was no mean effort even to get to this stage. The ditch at the Stones of Stenness is 2.3 m deep and at the bottom it is cut through the rock. The ditch at Brodgar is 3 m deep. We have to remember that people were working with Stone Age technology. There were no metal spades or picks available to help them, no mechanised pulleys for the removal of spoil. For shovels, people had bone tools; the scapula of a cow was commonly used, and picks would be made of bone or antler. Strong baskets would have been made to transport spoil, assisted no doubt by ropes.

It has been estimated that some 80,000 hours of work went into the construction of the ditch at the Ring of Brodgar (the removal of 4700 cubic metres of rock) and the figure for the Stones of Stenness (620 cubic metres of rock) is 12,500 hours (Figure 41).[6] To compare this with other sites, it has been estimated that construction of the later phases of the ditch at Avebury may have taken around 30 weeks and involved some 300 people.[7] The monument at Stonehenge, not far from Avebury, is complex and developed over a considerable period of time but construction of the early ditch may have taken some 11,000 hours of work,[8] while the shaping and erection of the megaliths for the later stages of the monument is likely to have taken considerably longer, perhaps involving a workforce of some 600 people and as many as 1.75 million person hours.[9] Estimates of time such as these are based on different criteria so they should not be regarded as precise. It is also the case that these monuments were not designed as unified entities in the way that we see them today, nor were any of them built in a single continuous process. The point is made, however, that henge-building required a considerable input of time as well as skill.

It may well have been that people returned on an annual basis to complete the monuments in short bursts. Similar sites elsewhere seem to have been built by individual gangs each contributing to a particular arc of ditch or set of stones.[10] These were farmers who had other duties and construction work would have to be fitted around that, though the mere fact that they could set aside the time to do this is a mark both of the success of their cultivation and of the importance of the task.

The raising of the stones

We do not know how soon after completion of the ditch the stones were erected but archaeologists tend to think that this task followed shortly afterwards. Certainly to our eyes the monuments look as if they were designed as an entity, though that may just be a reflection of a uniformity of purpose.

Given the general lack of detailed analysis of these sites it is difficult to detect the minute changes of plan that are likely to have arisen as they developed.

Suitable stone for the uprights is plentiful in Orkney. Some may have come from close at hand, but some of the best stone is to be found in the Sandwick area, about 12 km to the north. There are active quarries in this area today, and Colin Richards has been investigating one site at Vestrafiold, in the hills to the north of Skara Brae, where there is evidence for the extraction of standing stones. The stones from Vestrafiold seem to have been transported to the Ring of Brodgar, itself no mean feat in a Stone Age society. The use of local water courses would no doubt have facilitated the movement of the stones, as at Stonehenge, and local archaeologist Nick Card has identified two

FIGURE 40.
House 2 at Barnhouse.
RAYMOND PARKS

FIGURE 41.
The Stones of Stenness.
RAYMOND PARKS

A Perspective View of the Standing Stones in the Parish of Stainhouse in Orkney

FIGURE 42.

Bird's eye views of the Ness of Brodgar: (a) George Low drew this scene to illustrate his tour through the islands which was first published in 1774. It contains all sorts of fascinating detail such as the couple at the Odin Stone, and the ceremony in the churchyard; (b) A modern photograph tries to recapture the scene – interestingly Low, in his imagination, produced a view that is almost impossible to photograph. He visualised the monuments as closer together than they really are so that it is necessary to twist the camera and stitch two views together.

LOW: COURTESY OF THE ORKNEY LIBRARY AND ARCHIVE PHOTOGRAPHIC LIBRARY; PHOTOGRAPH: JOHN LEITH

prepared, but apparently unused, stones by the side of the loch to the north of the Ring of Brodgar.[11] We know nothing of the Neolithic language, but we can be fairly certain that a few choice swear words would have been heard when the stones slipped from their transport!

Before a stone could be raised the ground would have to be carefully prepared. This included the digging of a deep foundation, which must have extended into the bedrock. The standing stones as we see them comprise about two-thirds of the stone itself. The remaining third is below ground. In order to raise a stone, a system of timbers, ropes and perhaps turf would have to be set up. There have been various reconstructions in different places over the years and there were clearly different ways in which the raising of stones weighing some 30 tons could be achieved. One common element, however, whatever the precise mechanism, is the sheer amount of human muscle that would be required.

The standing stones were obviously an important element of the monuments, but they were not always erected on a grand scale. The Ring of Bookan, if it is a henge site, incorporates vertical stones on a much smaller scale. The lack of excavation here, however, means that it is difficult to incorporate it into a detailed understanding of how the peninsula worked.

The development of the peninsula

The scale of the monuments on the Brodgar peninsula is such that it is difficult for us to imagine the landscape as anything other than in its present state, with two large settings of standing stones and many smaller sites (Figure 42). It would not have looked like this at any time in prehistory, however. Not only were there other structures between the monuments, such as Barnhouse and Ness of Brodgar, but the main sites were not all built together and at first the numerous burial mounds were not there.[12]

Some of the earliest activity seems to have taken place 5,000 years ago, around Maeshowe, where there is increasing evidence for the construction of a ceremonial centre. The building of the tomb represents a shift of focus here as it became a house for the dead and the site of different ceremonies that may have included fewer people. A few generations later work began at the Stones of Stenness, perhaps also initially a ceremonial structure. Less is known about the creation of the Ring of Brodgar, but it started last, around 2500 BC. It is also worth remembering the sites at Bookan, though we do not yet understand how they fit into the overall picture.

The whole area was considered holy for many generations. Even after the original ways had changed, so that chambered tombs were no longer used, nor henge sites created, people still wanted to be buried in the vicinity of the great circles of the past. Colin Richards and his colleagues have pointed out that, though today we tend to focus on the upright stones and the sites as we see them, the actual acts of construction may well have been equally significant to those who originally designed and used the area.[13] The spread of activity across the peninsula was considerable, and sites were added and altered as necessary. The archaeological remains of today may well have arisen slowly and almost piecemeal. Their construction was a statement to the gods but it also served as a message for people. Knowledge of these sites must have extended beyond the communities who used them, even to the mainland of Scotland. The communities of Orkney were making a clear declaration of their wealth and leisure and of the intimacy of their relationship with the spiritual world (Figure 43).

It is interesting to note that the last monument to be built, the Ring of Brodgar, is the largest. Was this the culmination of centuries of prosperity and experience? Yet Brodgar today is apparently the simplest monument. It seems likely that a wealth of archaeological evidence must lie preserved below the fragile peaty capping of the interior, and also around the outside of the ditch.

Far afield folk?

The Brodgar peninsula was an important spot for Neolithic Orkney. Although standing stones were erected across Orkney, there is no concentration of sites quite like that on the peninsula, and it may well have formed a central place for the islands. There is widespread evidence for Neolithic communities across Orkney; would they all have been participants at Brodgar from time to time? It has so far been impossible to link any specific settlement or tomb site with any of the henge sites, but we know that the people of the time were accomplished travellers. Orkney is neither large nor treacherous for the traveller, and small boats would have made transport around Orkney relatively easy in the right weather conditions. It is thus certainly possible that on occasion people travelled across the islands to participate in the activities around Brodgar. Hard evidence is lacking but it is likely that the monuments that we have delegated as the Heart of Neolithic Orkney were indeed representative for the Neolithic population of the islands. Communities from near and far are likely to have travelled to join in both construction and worship at this place.

Participation in the ceremonies

What went on at the Ring of Brodgar, the Stones of Stenness, and the Ring of Bookan? We just do not know. The existence of ditches and low external banks suggests that boundaries were important. A space was set apart for ceremony, and it may well be that physical access was restricted to certain people, though the size of the sites suggests that more people would be involved than inside a chambered tomb. Indeed, none of the sites are the same size, and there are notable differences between each. Perhaps each served a different purpose.

At the heart of each site the preparation of a level circular platform invites ideas of community participation, especially given the size of the wide central area at Brodgar. It may be that the external bank provided access for viewing for those who could not enter. Access may have been dependent on age, gender or ancestry. It may have changed at different times of the year. Views into the circle seem to have been important, but so were views out. The geographical setting of these sites, at the heart of a great natural amphitheatre, has often been noted. Those who wove their spells inside the stones must have been very aware of the ring of low hills and the power of the sky that surrounded them.

The importance of the sky

The sky offers another clue to elements of the ceremonies that took place inside the circles. The importance of the winter solstice at Maeshowe has already been discussed. Elsewhere in Britain specific groups of standing stones have been associated with particular celestial events such as solstices or moonrise.[14] At the Stones of Stenness it is possible to watch the winter sun roll along the hills of Hoy between the two central surviving standing stones.[15] The tops of these stones seem to mimic the shape of those hills very closely in a way that is unlikely to be chance. Indeed it is hard not to look for significance in the sharply angled tops of each stone at both the Stones of Stenness and the Ring of Brodgar, though some stones have fractured and many have been re-erected in recent times (Figure 44).

The sky, both by day and by night, is of especial importance to any preliterate society that lives without the aid of clocks and calendars to mark the passing of the day and the turning of the seasons. This is especially so to those who do not have the bright light of electricity to obscure so much of the night sky and who were so much more vulnerable to the coming of adverse weather.

FIGURE 43.
Many of the standing stones are massive. This one, part of the Ring of Brodgar, was split by lightning in the 1980s.
RAYMOND PARKS

FIGURE 44.
The angled tops of the
standing stones seem to
have held a special
significance. Although
many of the stones at
the Ring of Brodgar
have been re-erected,
here at the Stones of
Stenness it is possible
to see how the shape of
the distant hills of Hoy
is reflected in the shape
of the angle.

RAYMOND PARKS

It is hard not to conclude that many of the ceremonies within the circles may have been designed to mark the rise or fall of particular stars or features that coincided with the change from one season to the next. Some have linked the Ring of Brodgar to lunar observation,[16] though this works best for the centuries around 1500 BC, long after the circle was first set up.[17] Others have pointed out that the traditional name for the ring, 'The Temple of the Sun', suggests that the aim was to ensure or mark the appearance of the sun over distant hills.[18] It is equally possible that other aspects of the natural world were important, such as winter storms that needed to be deflected as they approached, or rain that needed calling after a dry spell. One cannot but wonder at the effect of the 'merry dancers', the aurora, as it reached through the night sky over the stones on a crisp autumn evening.

In Britain today we know four seasons, but many societies divide their year into finer tranches of time, such as the Sámi, 'the people of eight seasons'.[19] The Neolithic inhabitants of Orkney may well have recognised a finer division of seasons than us and each would have its rituals, ceremonies and marker points in the landscape. The complexity and sophistication of the remains at the Heart of Neolithic Orkney suggests that different, but linked, activities took place, perhaps at different seasons of the year. The individual circles each mark different points of contact for land and sky, and these in turn change as the sun, moon, and stars pass through their individual cycles. We can only guess at what was important, but we can see that people were living within a sophisticated system of belief and action.

The different elements of ceremony

The ceremonies of the Neolithic community did not all look outwards, to propitiate the gods. Some activities focused internally on the community itself.

As a part of the belief system the bodies of the dead may have been bought into the circles of stone to ease their passage into the spirit world, celebrate their doings, or hasten their rebirth here on earth. Other elements of activity may have involved the new-born, couplings, or comings of age. Successful harvests were surely celebrated, as well as a particularly good fishing trip, or the coming of a trader with axes and hides from mainland Scotland.

Dance, music, and colour must all have played their part, though they have left little trace over the years. Archaeologists are just learning how to look for the wider elements of life away from the physical remains of stone and ditch construction. Work into the acoustic properties of some sites is just beginning,[20] but it is not hard to imagine the effect of chant, rhythm and tune inside a stone circle, especially if there were fires to enhance the setting. Sound is a powerful force, especially when it is combined with the coming together of the whole community or group.

Traces of pigment survive in bone pots at Skara Brae, and lumps of haematite were brought from Hoy in order to make decoration. We do not yet know whether the people were painting themselves, their clothes, their goods, or the standing stones. Perhaps paint could be applied everywhere. Dance is still more difficult to pin down. If there was rhythm there is likely to have been dance, and we may hear an echo of that across the ages in the many traditional stories that associate standing stones with dance and revelry. The rather monochrome world of archaeology was once more vivid.

The complexity of features at the Stones of Stenness, even in the small proportion that was excavated across the central platform, suggests that many different activities, on quite different scales, may have taken place here at different times.[21] They also show that the long-term use of individual sites was not static. Early activity at the Stones of Stenness may have focused on a ceremonial structure rather than the open circle. Nevertheless, the great henge sites were clearly important, though it is also likely that some things were celebrated at home. Neolithic houses share a very uniform layout and it is likely that this reflects elements of ritual. Religious life was tightly interwoven with everyday life so that small acts of belief were carried out on a daily basis.

The extent of the site

We can focus on the rings of standing stones and henge ditches that survive, but it is important to remember that they form only a part of a huge ceremonial site. Many ancillary sites, including standing stones, chambered tombs, and even houses fill the space between the best-preserved monuments. In effect, the site comprises the whole of the Brodgar peninsula,[22] and as such it dwarfs the individual areas designated as World Heritage Sites.

Immediately to the east of the Ring of Brodgar stands the isolated Comet Stone. Further to the south-east a pair of standing stones stands in the garden of Lochview Cottage, and the magnificent Watch Stone stands beyond them at the south point where the lochs join (Figure 45). Evidence for a second standing stone was found here during roadworks. The Stone of Odin stood between the Watch Stone and the Stones of Stenness, though it was destroyed in the early nineteenth century,[23] and beyond the stones, still in the same general alignment, the Barnhouse Stone stands alone in the field by the present main road. Some archaeologists have suggested that these stones may be the vestiges of a great stone avenue that once led along the peninsula. Avenues are well known from other sites such as Callanais in the Outer Hebrides, and Stonehenge and Avebury in the south of England, and the fertility of the land here on the peninsula has led to well-recorded dilemmas for local farmers who, in the past, were not always averse to removing any stones that stood in their way. Some stones have certainly been removed. Even today, agricultural work frequently exposes new archaeological material, and though the farming community is well acquainted with the interest of archaeology its patience must at times be tried! The search for further evidence for an avenue is one of the priorities for future work.

Others have put forward a more restricted interpretation of matched standing stones standing in pairs along the peninsula. Whatever its nature, a linear feature here would certainly have provided a processional way to complement the circular henge sites. Further support for this was added by geophysics work in 2004 which seems to suggest a linear trace running along the peninsula towards the meeting point of the waters of the lochs.[24]

A relationship with the land

Identification with the land is important for a farming community[25] and in Neolithic Orkney this was marked not just by the chambered tombs, but also by the stone settings. The stones themselves often match the prominent points of the horizon as it is viewed from within them. This is not just a question of looking out from the stones, however; it is also relevant to consider the stones as viewed from afar.

Standing stones tend to be in notable locations, often above water and visible from a long distance, especially in a landscape uncluttered by modern development. The great circles of the Ring of Brodgar and the Stones of Stenness are clearly visible from a wide circle of Mainland Orkney, even today. They must have stood out sharply in the Neolithic landscape. We cannot be sure whether they cemented the people of Orkney to the islands or simply acted as a centre for the West Mainland. The lack of other centres in the islands, and the size of this site, suggests the former.

Why the Brodgar peninsula?

Why was this place chosen? Obviously we do not know, but to even begin to answer that we have to look back in time to the roots of the Neolithic inhabitants of Orkney. The Ness of Brodgar incorporates many elements that we know were likely to be significant 5,000 years ago. It was a rich spot where the resources of fresh and salt water mingled. Seals frequently make their way from the sea into the warm shallow waters of the Loch of Stenness where they can doze on submerged boulders. Perhaps the first boatload of farmers came this way too, to find a safe harbour from which to explore. The land of the peninsula was fertile and already well known to those who lived there; there was much to harvest in the way of berries and other wild plants and it offered a good place to clear fields and till crops. Wildfowl abounded on both lochs.

From this place it was possible to see across Orkney – even if we imagine the gently wooded landscape that the first farmers encountered, which would have been so very different to that of today. By standing on the rise at Bookan, or at Brodgar, and looking out across the water of the lochs it would have been possible to see further than from most places. As the woodland disappeared and people began to shape the landscape the prominence of the spot becomes more imposing. Standing at the heart of the lochs today it is not hard to imagine oneself at the heart of Orkney. This is a special place.

The view was not just about the land, however. Water and sky were also important and the Ness of Brodgar offers a unique combination of all three. Those who stood here 5,000 years ago were at the centre of three significant elements: earth; sky; and water. If we add a fourth element – air – one can see that they were truly at the heart of their world. Even today the visitor to the Ring of Brodgar is aware of these elements.

These monuments are between the wind and the water.

FIGURE 45.
The Watch Stone.
C. WICKHAM-JONES

CHAPTER SEVEN

The Wider World of the Neolithic

There are many archaeological remains dating to the Late Neolithic across
Orkney. The World Heritage Sites have been set apart in the twenty-first
century on the grounds of their exceptional preservation, but they are by no
means unique. Before the rise of centralised centres of government and power
such as Kirkwall it is likely that both the northern and southern islands of the
Orkney archipelago were home to communities that flourished in similar
fashion to those on the Mainland of Orkney. In a society that did not require
mechanised transport, and the specialised tarmac roads that cost so much to
maintain in the outer islands today, Mainland had no particular advantage.
The Neolithic communities of the islands of Orkney were not constrained by
the needs of transport and infrastructure as we are. Transport may have been
more simple and slower, but it was also easier to maintain and operate.
Although some goods came in from the outside, individual communities across
the islands were self-sufficient.

Elsewhere in Orkney

Tombs

Other Neolithic village sites have been mentioned, but chambered tombs are
plentiful across the islands as well.[1] Most occur among the fertile lands which
make the islands of Orkney so green, some were built at the edge of the farmed
land. They are by no means confined to inhabited islands; a few were built on
tiny uninhabited skerries and islets.

All of the tombs include the same essential elements: a passage leading to a
chamber, all of which is covered by a mound. However, each has its own idiosyncrasies, as if to emphasise the individuality and needs of particular
communities. Some sites survive as grassy mounds, while others comprise a
mere handful of upright slabs. In general these tombs were well respected by
later communities who would seek to avoid damaging them with the plough
or robbing stones from them. Some, interestingly, were incorporated into later
structures, and this did not always include burial. The tomb at Pierowall
Quarry in Westray was incorporated into a broch in the Iron Age, some 2,500
years after the first bones of the local Neolithic population were laid to rest
there.

Some groups of tombs share particular characteristics. In Rousay there is a
series of well-preserved stalled cairns in which the external stonework has been

carefully laid to form a herringbone pattern around the outside of the cairn. There must have been a skilled stonemason working here who was able to pass on his craft and persuade the local communities that the inclusion of his hand-iwork would be a worthwhile element of their tomb design.

Although work in the past has often been preoccupied with the structures and contents of the tombs, archaeologists have always been concerned with their wider context.[2] This was developed by David Fraser whose study of the cairns in Rousay provided a more detailed social setting.[3] Recent trends in archaeology have bought this to the fore, both from the point of view of indi-vidual sites[4] and groups of sites.[5] Interestingly, though archaeologists concentrate on the locations where sites occur, a quick study of the distribu-tion maps of chambered tombs suggests that it might be profitable to look instead at the areas where they are not found.[6] Cummings and Pannett have developed the idea that some areas may have been set aside for the monuments of the dead,[7] which begs the question of what was going on elsewhere.

Settlement sites

The number of tombs gives an idea of the density of population in Neolithic Orkney. There are, in fact, many more tombs than settlement sites. One reason for this lies in the robust nature of the tombs; they stand prominent in the landscape and were generally respected in later times. Settlements, on the other hand, were less prominent in the first place and the individual houses were more prone to stone-robbing as material was taken for new buildings.

The exceptional preservation of Skara Brae is, in many ways, unusual. Skara Brae is likely to have been abandoned before the houses were buried in sand, but it looks as if the conditions that led up to the sand blow were such that life had become very difficult in the vicinity of the site. As the fields became exposed to increasing sand cover and salt spray coming in from the encroaching sea, so the crops became poorer. The people of Skara Brae had every reason to leave their settlement behind and start afresh in a less exposed position. This probably happened piecemeal, as different families gave up the struggle at different stages. They may not all have gone to the same place; with time people were living less in tight-knit villages, and settle-ment in the Bronze Age seems to have been more dispersed. At their new homes it may well have been easier to quarry new stone than return to collect the old, and there may have been a general feeling that the old houses were somehow unlucky. Today there are still parts of Orkney where houses are left when the owner dies or moves away, rather than sold or incorporated into a new dwelling.

The remains of the Neolithic houses at Barnhouse comprised little more than a couple of courses of stone and this is likely to be the condition of most surviving Neolithic settlements. This makes them much harder to find. Barnhouse was discovered by chance where it had begun to erode out at the side of the loch. Ness of Brodgar, which seems to have similar types of remains, among other finds, was uncovered during ploughing and at first it was thought to comprise the remains of a burial cist from the Bronze Age. Land that is good for the farmer of today was also valued in the past and no doubt there are other village sites in agricultural land such as this.

Skara Brae was not the only settlement that favoured the coast. There were no doubt attractions in the proximity of marine resources to complement those of the field, though these sites could be vulnerable to the elements. Other coastal settlements are known; many are now covered by sand, such as Noltland in Westray, Pool in Sanday and Howmae in North Ronaldsay (Figure 47). Few of these sites have been excavated and the details of everyday life are therefore lacking, but it is likely that their abandonment was a gradual process related to the slow incursion of the sea rather than to a series of individual catastrophes. As at Skara Brae any increase in wind from the sea, as protective dunes were worn back, would bring with it higher levels of salt spray and sand deposits so that the benefits of a coastal location disappeared. The fields gradually lost fertility and as it became more difficult to sustain a farm by the sea, so families gradually moved inland.

Ceremonial sites

If there are plentiful chambered tombs and some settlements from the Late Neolithic across Orkney, what about the ceremonial sites? Interestingly, no definite henge sites or stone circles have been recognised away from the heartland of the Ness of Brodgar. There are plenty of isolated standing stones, and these must have played an important role in the spiritual life of the community, but it is likely that people also looked elsewhere for a setting for their ceremonies. In this respect we are drawn back to the communal external performance areas incorporated into the designs of most chambered tombs[8] and to the suggestion that these tombs may well have served more as temples than as tombs.[9] The presence of human bone inside the chambers has coloured our interpretations of these sites. It is important to remember that in most cases only a very small proportion of the people who were in a community has ever been found in them (if indeed anything has survived at all). Furthermore, the human bone is nearly always only part of an assemblage from a tomb. Other material goods, and the bones of other species, are often just as abundant.

At a local scale it seems that a community would have used the settings provided by a chambered tomb, or tombs, for worship. In this way the ancestral elements of their lives meshed with the spiritual elements. Elsewhere in the neighbourhood they could gather with others at the site of a standing stone. Every so often they might make the journey across the islands to gather in great rituals at the sites along the Ness of Brodgar. These ceremonies had a functional aspect as well as a spiritual side: no doubt they provided useful opportunities for other types of contact, for trade, family partnerships, and meetings with relations from further off. The land between the lochs may well have been the Heart of Neolithic Orkney.

FIGURE 46.
Everyday tools for the
Neolithic farmers of
Orkney: (a) a Neolithic
bone mattock some
5,000 years old has
been fastened to a
modern, replica, haft to
give an idea of how it
might have been used;
(b) a stone ard point,
which would have been
mounted on the tip of
a wooden plough and
pushed by hand to till
the ground; (c) *opposite*
two fine Neolithic
maceheads of polished
stone, one in a modern
haft.

ORKNEY MUSEUMS
AND HERITAGE

The Neolithic landscape

The structures of Neolithic Orkney are highly visible to us in the twenty-first century, but the world of the Neolithic inhabitants of Orkney comprised more than their structures. The land around them provided the essential setting for their lives. As we have seen, the home territory of their ancestors was something that people both celebrated and upheld.

This relationship with the land included contrasting elements. On the one hand there was the domestic world of the farmer: fields to be cleared and crops to be tended. On the other hand there was the wild world of the hunter: the sea to be chanced and hills to be walked (Figure 48).

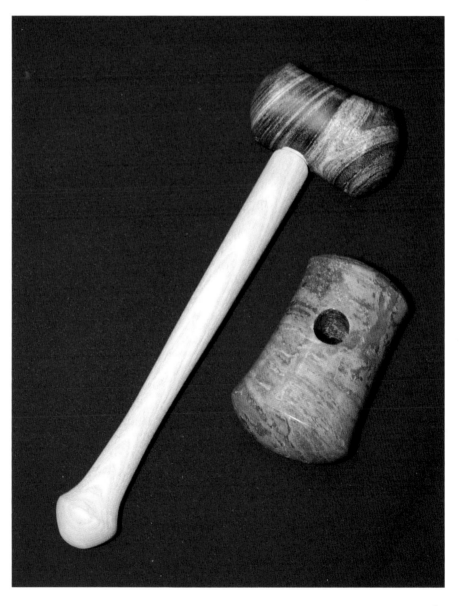

The taming of the land

The peoples of Mesolithic Orkney had a comprehensive knowledge of the land and they looked after it, but it was only in the Neolithic that the face of the land began to change. As farming spread people needed increasing space. They had to clear land for crops and to provide suitable grazing for their animals. The woodland cover was no longer advantageous and it began to be removed. As the trees disappeared the way was left open for the wind to enter and this speeded up the process of clearance.

It is impossible to overestimate the changes to the face of the land that took place at this time. In a confined space such as Orkney only a few centuries were needed for things to look very different. In place of small and shifting settlements of temporary structures, permanent stone farmsteads and villages began to appear. Fields were enclosed and surrounded by brushwood or low walls to keep animals out. Clearings of cropped grass became common and woodland receded. Well-trodden pathways appeared between the settlements as people moved from place to place both individually and in groups. There were goods to trade, and festivities to be organised. Marriage partners might visit family, and young adults would have sought new lands to settle. Tombs were built, often in prominent places, and henges and standing stones marked the locations where once a particular tree or boulder had indicated the work of the gods. For the first time the land was held down under a web of human making.

The fear of the wild

It is not surprising that the archaeological evidence suggests that the Mesolithic way of life quickly disappeared once farming became the norm. The economic changes led to a new material culture that included both large and small elements: from houses to everyday goods such as pottery. Concomitant social changes meant that communities no longer split and shifted and moved across the land. Advancing techniques in biomolecular archaeology [10] are opening up new suites of evidence that show how diet changed as the farmers relied more on the meat from their animals and less on marine resources. [11] The analysis of residues on pottery indicates the use of milk and dairy products for the first time. [12] Studies of ancient DNA may even be able to pinpoint the movement of people across Britain as the agricultural techniques spread. [13]

The shifts in society had physical expressions that are reflected in the archaeological record, but they went further than that. The accumulated evidence suggests that the adoption of agriculture also bought strong new spiritual elements. Ian Hodder was one of the first to explore the changes in attitude that took place with the change in lifestyle [14] and this has led to some interesting discussion, most recently by Richard Mabey. [15]

It may well be that the arrival of farming provided the catalyst for people to begin to feel displaced from the world. Prior to this people lived in careful symbiosis with a whole living system that incorporated all the elements of the world around them from the sun to rivers, rocks, plants and animals. [16] With the adoption of agriculture the focus of concern changed, and became orientated towards the land: the soil on which they depended for sustenance. For the first time communities had the power to change the world around them, but they also had the awareness that it could change them. Careful farming would lead to well-stocked fields and a good winter. But no one could do anything about a bad storm that might lead to a flattened crop and famine. The well-being of society depended on being able to provide enough food for everyone. Life was still balanced on a knife edge and it was not always in the power of the people to ensure that things went their way. They were only too aware of the power of nature.

The inevitable rolling past of the seasons may also have taken on new significance at this time. In Orkney a bad, or shorter, summer would have a serious adverse effect on harvest (not to mention those who had to work out in it). It is interesting to note how many of our myths of paradise consider a place where it is always spring, where seasonal fluxes are lessened.[17]

In twenty-first-century Britain we are just beginning to rediscover the value of wild land and the power of the elements. The desire to tame the land, and thus be sure of it, may well have originated among our Neolithic ancestors some 5,000 years ago. We have only just begun to realise that we harness, or alter, the natural balance of the world at our peril.

Beyond Orkney

Late Neolithic sites occur across Scotland and, of course, elsewhere in Britain. In general there is less evidence for settlement, because of the use of timber for domestic buildings away from Orkney. The houses were there, but their traces are harder to spot. In recent years, however, archaeology has improved its techniques of recognising the traces of early timber buildings, and excavations of Neolithic house sites are on the increase. As research continues so the picture of Neolithic Britain slowly emerges.

There were other great centres of ceremonial activity in Neolithic Britain that complemented the Brodgar peninsula. Callanais, in the Outer Hebrides,[18] Kilmartin, in west Scotland,[19] and Thornborough, in north Yorkshire,[20] are all similar centres, each with its own particular characteristics. An especially vibrant centre seems to have existed in Wessex, in southern England.[21] Here the great sites of Stonehenge and Avebury form prominent elements of a huge complex of monuments that included circular henges, long avenues, chambered tombs, and varied settings of timber and stone uprights. In Ireland a similar complex was created at the Bend of the Boyne[22] and included all the familiar elements: a henge site; impressive chambered tombs; and varied settings, again with their own individual characteristics.

Neolithic Orkney is undoubtedly important to twenty-first-century archaeologists (see Chapter Eleven), and it was undoubtedly a flourishing part of north-west Europe in the fourth millennium BC. It was, however, just one part of a society that spread across a wide geographical area, albeit with localised

FIGURE 47.
Excavations at the
Neolithic site of the
Links of Noltland,
Westray in the 1980s.
C. WICKHAM-JONES

idiosyncrasies. The preservation of archaeological remains in Orkney may be exceptional, but Gordon Barclay has argued convincingly that we should not let the local vagaries of survival mislead us into setting areas such as Orkney or Wessex apart.[23] Equally interesting communities flourished in the rest of Britain and it is one challenge for future archaeologists to seek them out.

The Neolithic in the twenty-first century

One curious aspect of these great Neolithic sites lies in the number that has been designated as World Heritage Sites today. It is surely a tribute to our Neolithic ancestors, and a mark of their sophistication, that their sites have come to play such an important role in the life of the twenty-first century. The Bend of the Boyne, Stonehenge and Avebury, and the Heart of Neolithic Orkney have all been included on the World Heritage List, and there are other Neolithic World Heritage Sites elsewhere in Europe. These are popular places to visit that require careful management to lessen the pressures that we place upon them. One element of this management is to ensure that as many people as possible understand how these sites might have been used in the past and the role that they have played through the centuries (Figure 49).

FIGURE 48.
Orkney landscape:
view across the
Sound of Hoy.
SIGURD TOWRIE

FIGURE 49.
The Stones of Stenness
with their World
Heritage Plaque.

C. WICKHAM-JONES

CHAPTER EIGHT

The People After:
The Bronze Age and the Iron Age

Bronze Age Orkney

By 2000 BC farming was well established as a way of life in Orkney. The settlement at Skara Brae had probably been abandoned for almost 500 years, but the complex of monuments along the Brodgar peninsula was well developed and still well used. The population of Orkney was thriving, but change was in the air.

Changes to the way of life

The most obvious material change was the introduction of a brand new material – metal – but this was just one manifestation of a suite of changes that affected not only the way of life but also the beliefs of the people. The first copper and bronze objects must have been imported into Orkney from the south. There were other changes to the material culture at the time, and it has been argued that the new ways were bought in by incomers from across the North Sea.[1] The evidence is still unclear, because it does not seem that there was any great population change, while it is of course possible for ideas and goods to spread without the widespread movement of people. It is likely, however, that one of the new elements to which society had to adapt was the rise of a mobile class of travelling metalsmiths who guarded the secrets of the new metals carefully. There had, of course, been travellers before, even travelling tradesmen who could supply axe roughouts, hides, salt, and other necessities, but the role of the metalsmith is likely to have been slightly different. Even in historical times travelling smiths were regarded with a mixture of awe and fear, and it is not hard to see how the apparently magical transformations involved in the application of their craft might lead to this.

The other changes to material culture included the introduction of new styles of pottery: the so-called 'Beaker vessels', made of fine materials, in a slender design and covered with detailed decoration.[2] Beakers are very different to the coarse, bucket-shaped Grooved Ware pottery that had been fashionable in the Late Neolithic. Archery became important once again, and there were new styles of flint arrowhead and other pieces of equipment (Figure 50). These changes went hand in hand with considerable shifts in community values. Skills were gradually becoming more specialised, so that the community had to be able to provide an agrarian surplus to support those who supplied goods for their more specialised needs. The scene was set for the acquisition of personal wealth. Metal goods no doubt were expensive and available to only a few, but substitutes made of materials like red-coloured flint and carefully fashioned to approximate copper have been found. Gradually, across Scotland, emphasis shifted towards a rise in the importance of the individual.[3]

All of this combined to produce a significant change that may have gone unnoticed by the people of the day. Not only were there, for the first time, people who had belongings that others could only aspire to. Even more importantly, for the first time individual communities were no longer quite so self-sufficient. The demand for metal required materials and skills that were not readily available among the local population.

From village to steading
Bronze Age settlement remains in Orkney have only been recognised in any number in recent years.[4] There was a general trend away from nucleated villages to dispersed farmsteads and this has made the traces of Bronze Age houses difficult to spot, but the introduction of intensive research and better geophysical prospection means that more sites are being found.

By the time of the Bronze Age sea level change around Orkney seems to have slowed down and the coasts approximated their present positions, though recent research indicates that there is a small relative rise in sea level still taking place today.[5] During the Bronze Age settlement seems to have been moved away from the coast. Coastal sites like Skara Brae were often abandoned by this time, others declined into single farmsteads. Elsewhere, settlement expanded into upland areas that had previously been left empty. This was no doubt partly due to the success of the farming communities who would need more and more ground as they increased in size. It would be compounded by the fashion for dispersed steadings which meant that people had to seek out new lands in their search for somewhere to live. A benign climate at the time made this possible, but it was a short-lived development. Many Bronze Age homesteads were soon to be abandoned as the climate became cooler and wetter[6] and the marginal uplands turned to moorland; farming was no longer viable in these locations. Tofts Ness, at the northern tip of Sanday, is a good example of an area that was intensively settled and cultivated in the Bronze Age, though it is outside the agricultural lands of today.[7]

Bronze Age settlement often comprised small round houses and today many appear as simple hut circles. These comprise the circular foundations of stone on which low walls of turf would have been capped by thatched roofs. Some dwellings, such as the house at Wasbister, to the north-west of the Ring of Brodgar, were more complex, however. Detailed geophysics at Wasbister has revealed a small farmstead comprising at least two circular structures with a complex of field enclosures and possibly trackways that lead away (Figure 51).[8] Excavations at Crossiecrown, not far from the coast on the Bay of Firth, have

uncovered a house which seems to have many Late Neolithic features, though it is of Early Bronze Age date.[9]

Other Bronze Age sites are marked by low mounds of burnt stone and contain abundant evidence of the use of fire and heat. These sites are known as 'burnt mounds' and they have been interpreted as the result of many activities, from domestic cooking to saunas or feasting sites. Some do appear to be associated with dwellings and may simply be the remains of domestic activities, but others lack the general detritus of everyday life and have more complicated structures incorporating great tanks that appear to have held water. These are likely to have had a different purpose. Burnt mounds are common across the Orkney landscape, though they are by no means all Bronze Age; they are associated with dates from the Neolithic right through to the medieval period.

Farming and the landscape

The farmers of Bronze Age Orkney maintained their fields carefully and this had an effect on the soil. Fossil soils at Tofts Ness, Sanday, have been found to contain evidence for intensive cultivation and manuring.[10] There is evidence for considerable land enclosure at the time, from individual field walls to the larger 'treb dykes' which stretch for many miles across islands such as Sanday. Crops included wheat, barley, and oats; and animals, especially cattle, were important.

Later in the Bronze Age, from around 1100 BC a climatic downturn made life difficult across the whole of Britain.[11] Rainfall increased and temperatures dropped and, as a result, many of the higher farms had to be abandoned, leading to the large numbers of hut circles that litter our hills and moorlands. One incidental result of this has been the occasional preservation of fragile

FIGURE 50.
Bronze Age artefacts:
(a) a small food vessel,
similar to those often
placed with cremations;
(b) a fine flint
arrowhead.

ORKNEY MUSEUMS
AND HERITAGE

92

artefacts from the Bronze Age in the numerous bogs and mires that developed across the countryside from this time on.

The wooden yoke which was preserved in White Moss, in Shapinsay, is thought to date from this period, as is the wooden replica of a Bronze Age sword found in a bog in Tankerness in 1957. This find, the Groatsetter sword, is of particular interest; though the original owner could not apparently afford a bronze sword, it would still have been necessary to import rare yew wood from the south for this object. Or perhaps it was important for this piece to be made of wood? Whatever the significance of the material, the weapon itself seems to have held considerable meaning. Although the blade was apparently fresh, the hilt looked as if it had been worn from much use. The location of both artefacts in bogland suggests that they may have been deliberately deposited, perhaps as gifts to the gods or as an act of placation, possibly against increasing rain. There is evidence across Europe that bogs and watery places were important centres for ritual deposits from this time and into later millennia.[12]

The rise of the individual

As people had to leave the marginal lands competition for the fertile lower land increased. Greater population pressure meant that it was even more important for the individual to demonstrate social dominance. The introduction of metal and other changes to material goods offered ample opportunity for this. Metal, of course, lent itself admirably to weapons and ostentatious objects of show and this is precisely how it turns up in the archaeological record.

This concern with material things seems to have been combined with other shifts in society. The gradual loss of self-sufficiency has been noted above, but at a basic level people were still producing the greater part of their everyday needs. Deeper changes in people's attitude to the spiritual world were, however, evident; changes, in both ceremony and burial, are seen in the archaeological record.

Burial

The burial record of Bronze Age Orkney is geared towards individual burials.[13] The practice of communal interment disappeared. Some chambered tombs fell out of use at this time, but many were still regarded as holy places and they were adapted for the new requirements of society. There seems to have been a period of rebuilding and alteration at many sites. At many tombs the entrances were blocked and, though ceremonies still took place, there must have been important differences in the activities carried out. There are deposits of Beaker pottery from several of the Orkney chambered tombs that must have been laid down at this time.

Burial itself took place in a variety of ways and was often carried out away from the chambered tombs. Burial mounds (earthen barrows) were popular, usually containing a single primary grave, though later graves were often added. Many burial mounds are quite modest in size compared to the previous

FIGURE 51.
The Bronze Age house
at Wasbister is just
visible as a low mound
in the centre of this
picture. On the horizon
stands the Ring of
Brodgar.
SIGURD TOWRIE

chambered tombs, but some maintain the tradition of erecting a prominent monument. Four prominent burial mounds surround the Ring of Brodgar, but perhaps the most impressive barrow cemetery in Orkney is that at the Knowes of Trotty, less than ten kilometres to the east.

There are 12 huge barrows at the Knowes of Trotty, many raised on top of natural hillocks to enhance their size. The largest barrow lies to the north and excavation of this mound in the nineteenth century revealed a rich cremation burial in a cist containing four gold discs with amber pendants and beads.[14] Recent excavation has shown how the visible barrows are only part of the site. Traces of a substantial stone structure were uncovered here alongside the remains of other settings, pyres and less prominent burials.[15] It seems that activity at the Knowes of Trotty included various ceremonies to do with the disposal of the dead as well as the construction of their actual resting places (Figure 52).

Jane Downes, of Orkney College, who conducted the excavations at Knowes of Trotty, has been researching the Bronze Age burials of Orkney and she has recorded some 550 barrows across Orkney, in 229 burial mound sites.[16] In addition there are many flat cemeteries, as well as unmarked graves, which are obviously only found by chance and so tend to be under-represented. The treatment of the dead varied greatly; some bodies were inhumed, others cremated, some were buried in pits, some in rocky pockets, some in cists. Cists might be alone, or under a barrow, and some cists were inserted into pre-existing barrows. Many burials were accompanied by grave goods; pottery survives most frequently, but stone tools are also found and evidence from elsewhere in Scotland suggests that food and drink may have been supplied for the dead.

Ceremony

The focus of spiritual life in the Bronze Age was still based around the same ceremonial sites that had been used in preceding centuries. In addition to work on the tombs, many sites were added to and adapted in this period. Although they were clearly still regarded as holy, the monuments obviously needed new elements to fulfil Bronze Age requirements, and the tradition of building with massive stones did not diminish. This must have been a phase of considerable building work. Many of the single standing stones around Orkney may have been erected at this time, and the Brodgar peninsula continued to act as an important central place. People still gathered for worship at the Stones of Stenness and the Ring of Brodgar, and they may well have gone on raising stones here.

Transport and change

Previous research on Bronze Age Scotland has suggested that in comparison to developments elsewhere, Orkney was slow to change, perhaps even conservative, in the Bronze Age. More recent research suggests that this may be a misconception, the result of the very great emphasis that has been placed on the study of Orkney's Neolithic monuments by archaeologists in the past. The remains of Bronze Age Orkney are certainly more elusive than those of Neolithic Orkney, but more refined techniques of survey are showing that they are plentiful. One problem is that at some sites, such as the monumental stone circles, the construction and design techniques used in the Bronze Age are not that different to those of the Neolithic. Monoliths of stone were still raised, smaller stone structures still erected and used; the findings are only to be differentiated according to the type of material goods found there. Archaeologists look for sherds of tell-tale Bronze Age pottery or stone tools and these are often scarce, or mixed in with earlier material.

FIGURE 52.
The burial mounds at
the Knowes of Trotty.
C. WICKHAM-JONES

The climatic downturn towards the end of the Bronze Age made life difficult, but people still invested considerable effort in the spiritual world.
Worship at the standing stone sites may have become more important as the
Bronze Age population of the islands tried to propitiate their gods and ask
for improved weather. And despite environmental difficulties, the finds from
the Knowes of Trotty show that some individuals were still able to amass
considerable wealth.

Nor was Orkney isolated in the Bronze Age. Metal goods, the first Beaker
pottery, and the new trappings of archery all came into the islands from
outside. The existing transport routes of the Neolithic must have facilitated
these links, and no doubt new networks were set up. Water transport was
still important and it is interesting that elsewhere in Britain the earliest
wrecks of trading ships date from the Bronze Age, including a find made off
the coast of Devon in 2005.[17] It is likely that metalwork continued to arrive
by sea because, though copper does exist in Orkney there is, as yet, no
evidence for prehistoric copper mines here. Very little evidence for local
metalworking in the Bronze Age has been found at all and Orkney lacks tin,
the vital ingredient to turn copper into bronze. The fine metal goods from
the Knowes of Trotty provide one hint of links to the south, as they show
influence in both design and manufacture from the rich Wessex area of
southern England. The gold discs and amber beads here are paralleled by
finds from Bush Barrow near to Stonehenge. Metal goods may have been
rare, but the communities of Orkney were not impoverished or backward in
the Bronze Age.

FIGURE 53.
Two of the stones at
the Ring of Brodgar
with the burial mound
of Fresh Knowe behind
them.
SIGURD TOWRIE

Skara Brae was abandoned by the Bronze Age, though one possible burial mound just inland of the site suggests that people may still have been in the area. Elsewhere, the Brodgar peninsula remained an important focus of activity. There may have been alterations and new settings at the henge sites themselves, but the most notable remains from the Bronze Age comprise the numerous burial mounds scattered across the peninsula. In the Bronze Age it was obviously very popular to be buried in close proximity to the earlier sites.

A total of nine burial mounds were recorded around Maeshowe in 1934, though only one is visible today. Six mounds were recorded around the Stones of Stenness in the nineteenth century, though none remain. Around the Ring of Brodgar, however, four impressive mounds survive. Each has a hollow summit, testimony to antiquarian work in the nineteenth century; there are some recorded details of finds and the make-up of these mounds, but there has been no recent work to corroborate, or extend, this evidence. These great mounds suggest important burials; they are complemented by at least nine smaller barrows to the south of the henge as well as geophysical signals that suggest other associated remains (Figure 53).

The barrows continue to the north of the Ring of Brodgar as far as Bookan. An unusual disc barrow lies in the lower ground by the side of the Loch of Stenness, and as the ground rises towards Bookan a series of mounds may be seen on the skyline. Some of the barrows once recorded here have been removed by the plough, but several survive, together with the large mound of Skae Frue, which was excavated by Thomas in the nineteenth century. He found three cist burials here.

In addition to the barrow cemeteries along the peninsula, many unmarked cist burials have been found over the years. Clusters of cists seem to have been located both near to the farm of Brodgar, and at Bookan, and there are indications that there may also have been unmarked cremation burials in pits rather than in cists.

There is also recent evidence relating to settlement from the Brodgar peninsula. At Wasbister, to the south of the Ring of Bookan, low earthworks indicate the survival of another archaeological site. For many years opinion varied as to whether this represented the remains of small cairns or round houses. Recent geophysical work has shown it to comprise the remains of a large double house dating to the Bronze Age and not unlike many Bronze Age houses from Shetland. We can now see that the Wasbister house lies at the centre of an extensive complex of settlement and farming remains.[18]

Between the Wasbister house and the Ring of Brodgar to the south lies the Dyke of Sean, a low dyke that marks the medieval parish boundary between Stenness and Sandwick. Archaeologists now think that there is a possibility that this earthwork dates back to the Bronze Age. If so it is not unusual; earthwork boundaries of similar date have been recorded elsewhere in the islands.

Iron Age Orkney

Sometime in the early first millennium BC, new goods began to make their way into Orkney in increasing numbers. These included iron knives as well as a range of new-fangled weapons. Swords, previously a rarity, became more important. Although archaeologists tend to concentrate on the things that differentiate the Iron Age from the preceding Bronze Age, in many ways life in this period reflected more continuity than change and developed naturally from what had gone before (Figure 54).

From steading to village

The dispersed settlement of the Bronze Age continued in the Iron Age, but villages are once again found in the archaeological record, and became more important with time. The isolated house sites of Iron Age Orkney often comprise substantial circular dwellings known as Atlantic round houses.[19] These were subdivided inside into separate rooms using the versatile Orkney flagstones, which could be moved as needed. Visiting some of the Iron Age settlements today, such as the houses that surround the Broch of Gurness, one gets the impression that the use of flagstones provided an early pre-fab: a house that could be adapted to the changing needs of the nuclear family.

As time passed some of the round houses were surrounded by defensive walls and ditches; competition for land remained intense and this led to social unrest. Out of these defended settlements a particular and notable structure seems to have developed – the broch. Brochs comprise circular towers of stone with an internal space for living and galleries in the walls.[20] A few may have been as much as 13 m tall, though many were lower. On the outside they were windowless and they must have appeared cheerless and daunting to those who approached. Brochs have often been seen as the ultimate answer to settlement in an aggressive society,[21] though this is still a controversial view (Figure 55).

In Orkney many brochs are surrounded by the remains of villages of low stone-built houses with defensive ditches around the whole. The broch provided a clear focus for the settlement, often with a grand entranceway, as at Gurness (Figure 56), and it may well have been the dwelling of a social elite. It has been suggested that Iron Age Orkney was socially more sophisticated than the rest of Scotland and it may have been that population pressure on the restricted but fertile land of the islands meant that more centralised forms of settlement and society had to develop.[22]

Away from the brochs, the presence of otherwise ephemeral house traces is sometimes indicated by the existence of a well-built stone souterrain. Souterrains are stone-lined tunnels, often leading to a sub-circular under-ground chamber. Many are known across Orkney, and new souterrains are still being found, usually when a heavy tractor sinks into one.[23] They are commonly interpreted as having been used for storage and often led out from the inside of a house.[24] Souterrains continued in use into the first millennium AD and they are part of a growing body of evidence that underground structures played

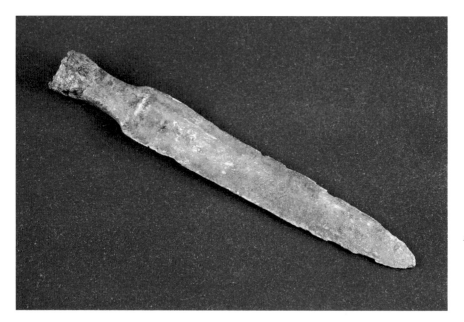

FIGURE 54.
Knife from Skaill,
Deerness. This knife
dates from the Bronze
Age levels at Skaill and
is the earliest known
metal artefact from
Orkney.
ORKNEY MUSEUMS
AND HERITAGE

an important role in the Iron Age. They may also have served a ritual function and this is the focus of current research by Martin Carruthers.[25]

Increasing defence

Life in the Iron Age was adapted to a time of general uncertainty and warfare between neighbours. Elsewhere in Scotland Iron Age settlement includes a range of hillforts and promontory forts. The restricted geographical area of the islands of Orkney, combined with their generally gentle topography, means that hillforts were, by and large, impractical. It may have been that the broch settlements took their place and provided all the defence that was needed, but the coast offered plenty of scope for well-defended promontory settlements.

FIGURE 55.
The broch at Gurness,
surrounded by the
remains of houses and
an outer defensive wall
and ditch.
SIGURD TOWRIE

FIGURE 56.
The entrance to
Gurness.

C. WICKHAM-JONES

Promontory forts are known from Orkney, such as those at the Brough of
Deerness or the Brough of Burgh Head in Stronsay, but few have been studied
in detail. None have obvious Iron Age marker finds, and some archaeologists
consider them to be more recent, but the possibility that some date back to
the Iron Age should be borne in mind.

Another type of site that is common in Iron Age Scotland but little studied in Orkney is the crannog. Crannogs comprise lake dwellings; they may be sited on existing islands or on artificial platforms. Some have been interpreted as defensive; others may have been situated in this way to maximise the area of productive arable land that was available. There are several potential crannog sites in Orkney but research into them is only just beginning. One crannog site at Breetaness in Rousay has been shown to have been occupied in the Iron Age, and a similar early date also seems likely for the crannog at Voy in the Loch of Stenness, which has been the subject of recent research by Bobby Forbes and Nick Dixon (Figure 57).[26]

Intensive cultivation and use of resources

The environment of the Iron Age farmers in Orkney was much like that of today. Agriculture continued to intensify along the lines that had begun in the Bronze Age.[27] Grain was cultivated, but stock increased in importance. Intensive animal husbandry led to the availability of increased manure for fertilisation. Orkney farmers had long known the value of adding minerals from domestic refuse to the land but manuring practices seem to have developed in the Iron Age and many farm mound sites have started at this time. Farm mounds are often still built on today; they occur where the modern steading sits on top of a low mound which has built up from previous farm refuse. They are to be seen especially in the northern isles such as Sanday. Recent research has confirmed that the heart of the mound is frequently based around Iron Age remains some 2,000 years old, and some may be older.[28]

As agriculture continued to expand across the landscape, so the importance of wild resources diminished, except as a resource to be used in time of need. Elsewhere in Scotland, the evidence suggests that activities like hunting continued to be important in Iron Age society, but wild remains seem to decrease in the archaeological record in Orkney. Excavations by Beverley Ballin Smith at the Howe, outside of Stromness, found evidence for decreasing numbers of red deer.[29] They were an important resource, and were used for not only for meat, but also for hides and antler. However, the red deer population was apparently extinct in the islands by the end of the Iron Age; the restricted geography of the islands, together with the needs of the rising population, may have been contributory factors to its demise. Although antler continued to be used to make articles such as combs, from the Iron Age onwards it had to be imported into Orkney.

Island skills and imported goods

Iron Age Orkney did not lose contact with the world outside, and there is evidence that at this time new skills were also being introduced into the islands.[30] Increasingly, remains of Iron Age metalworking are coming to light. Recent excavations at the Howe, near to Stromness, Mine Howe, in Tankerness, and Berstness, in Westray, have all yielded artefacts related to the manufacture of metal goods, such as moulds and smelting ovens (Figure 58).

These local smiths must have been using scrap metal and imported materials to get their raw material because there is no evidence for the prehistoric extraction of iron ore in Orkney, though it is to be found in Hoy.

There was increased local specialisation in other crafts in the Iron Age. The manufacture of fine goods was encouraged by the desire for individual wealth which might often be expressed through display. In addition to the metalwork, isolated finds such as the Orkney Hood demonstrate the skills of Iron Age craftsfolk. This comprises an elaborately made hooded cloak, apparently designed for a child, which was found in 1867 in a bog on Tankerness. It was thought to be medieval until a dating programme carried out by the National Museums of Scotland revealed that it was actually some 1,750 years old. We cannot be sure whether the Orkney Hood was lost by chance, but its location in a peat bog where other unusual artefacts have been recovered suggests that it may have been ritually deposited. Interestingly, the hood was not new when it was deposited; research by Jacqui Wood suggests that it had been carefully repaired and altered.[31]

Although many of the needs of the native population could be catered for locally, many imported goods have been unearthed during excavations from the sites of this time. At Howe a fine metal brooch in the shape of an insect was found in the later layers, alongside other imported goods such as beads and fragments of glass vessels. The elite of Iron Age Orkney clearly had access to fashionable and luxury goods from the south and it is not hard to imagine the travelling traders who would have brought cargoes of fine wares into the islands. Interestingly, there is an early account of the trading of fine woollen hoods out of Orkney and it is likely that the traders did not return empty-handed.

Later in the Iron Age finds from Orkney include Roman objects that had made their way north. Fragments of a Roman amphora were discovered at the broch of Gurness, though whether it was imported for the luxuries it originally contained, such as olive oil, sweet almonds, or wine, we can never know. A fine intaglio of carnelian carved with an eagle was found during the excavations at the Howe outside of Stromness. It had once been set into a ring and must have come from the south, but by the time the stone was lost the ring had disappeared.

Burial
Domestic life in the Iron Age offered plenty of scope to express personal status for those who could afford it. Was this carried through into the afterlife? Until recently evidence for Iron Age burial in the islands was scarce.[32] This has all changed with information from two on-going excavations, at Berstness (Figure 59), in Westray, and Mine Howe, in Mainland Orkney. Berstness is a complex site which seems to incorporate a structure that may have been used purely for ritual.[33] Around this structure the remains of other stone-built buildings have been used as a rubble base into which many burials were set. The burials comprise articulated skeletons and it is likely that the dead were

FIGURE 57.
The crannog at Voy:
the remains of the
causeway running out
to the island may
clearly be seen.
SIGURD TOWRIE

FIGURE 58.
The excavation of a
small metalworking
oven at Mine Howe.
ORKNEY
ARCHAEOLOGICAL
TRUST

FIGURE 59.
Excavations by EASE
at the Knowe of Skea,
Berstness 2004.

SIGURD TOWRIE

laid to rest here not long after death. Both men and women were buried at Berstness, but what is remarkable is that over 50 per cent of the skeletons are those of newborn babies and very young children. This cemetery lies on an isolated skerry, well away from any settlement remains. This may explain the lack of Iron Age burial elsewhere in Orkney, for if bodies were laid to rest in less favourable conditions little would survive to the present.

At Mine Howe,[34] the excavation of an elaborate ritual site has uncovered a complex of stone-built structures, evidence of metalworking and at least two skeletons. Cist burial also continued into the Iron Age and, though there is some evidence that long cists were starting to be adopted at this time, it may be that some of the unmarked and undated cist burials thought to be of Bronze Age date are in fact Iron Age. Both inhumation and cremation continued, sometimes in low cairns surrounded by a kerb. It seems that Iron Age burials continued to express the individuality of the dead, though this was often in a communal setting.

Ceremony and belief

What of the other expressions of religious life in the Iron Age, the ceremonies for the living? Until recently a lack of evidence from Orkney meant that information relating to Iron Age belief had to come from elsewhere. However, the study of the well-preserved underground structure at Mine Howe has prompted a reassessment of many other subterranean structures across Orkney and snatches of information are emerging. Mine Howe itself comprises a carefully built chamber set deep under the present ground surface and reached by two flights of steps that wind down into the ground. A combination of excavation and geophysics has shown that Mine Howe is surrounded by a deep

ditch and, associated with this, there was a complex of structures that included
workshops for metalworking. Mine Howe may have combined ritual and craftwork in a way that seems alien today, but it was undoubtedly an important
centre (Figures 60 and 61).[35]

The underground features of Mine Howe resemble those from other
Orkney sites such as the 'wells' found at some of the brochs, for example that
at Gurness.[36] In addition, there are the enigmatic souterrains, and stories of
other underground structures abound in the islands. This has prompted
archaeologists to revise their opinions and suggest that religion and ceremony
in the Iron Age may well have been articulated, partly at least, through underground activity. If so, the size of these features suggests that access was limited
so, as in the Neolithic, priestly intermediaries would have been important.
Ritual for the rest of the population may well have taken place near to the
entrances, perhaps in a more domestic setting.[37]

Mine Howe itself seems to have been a special place. Fire was undoubtedly
important there, for the transformation of the metal goods that were worked
if nothing else, and there are interesting connections with water and marsh in
the nearby bogs. The rising importance of boggy places has been noted from
the Bronze Age and this seems to have been developed into the Iron Age.
Mine Howe thus has many of the ingredients through which the spirit
world of the Iron Age may well have been manifest. Whether other sites such
as Mine Howe are to be found across Orkney we do not know; it may be that
in the Iron Age the focus for prehistoric Orkney had shifted away from the
fertile lands of Stenness and Brodgar to the wilder marshes of Tankerness and
St Andrews.

The later Iron Age and the Romans

During the first millennium AD domestic life in Orkney took place in the
context of a highly centralised society based around the broch settlements,
though isolated farms also existed. Further south, in England and southern
Scotland, life for many people was transformed by the incursion of the Roman
Empire. The Romans were certainly periodically interested in extending their
dominions throughout Scotland, but there is little evidence that they made any
great impact on Orkney. Tacitus records that the emperor Agricola sent his
fleet around Britain in circa AD 80, during which trip the Orcades were found
and conquered. There is no archaeological evidence for this, but it is an indication that the Romans knew of the islands. Occasional Roman artefacts turn
up on the sites of the time, such as Gurness, and a few may indicate that fine
goods were directly imported, while others merely represent the end of a long
chain of exchange, trade and influence.[38]

The World Heritage Sites in the Iron Age

The Iron Age finally saw the apparent abandonment of the great ceremonial
centres along the Brodgar peninsula and a wholesale shift of both religious
belief and the geographical focus of that belief. Some activity at the Stones of

FIGURE 60.
OAT excavations at the
circular structure at
Mine Howe.
ORKNEY
ARCHAEOLOGICAL
TRUST

Stenness is indicated by a few finds of Iron Age pottery from amongst the stones and central platform, but there is no archaeological evidence that the site was still a main focus for ceremony. The lack of excavation at the Ring of Brodgar means that any similar information has yet to be found.

The peninsula was not completely abandoned, however. The fertile soils of the area still exerted a strong pull and the remains of two possible broch sites have been recorded. Big Howe, immediately to the south-east of the Stones of Stenness, was recorded as a broch when it was flattened in the early 1900s, and this has been supported by geophysics across the low mound which is all that survives. A few hundred metres to the north a large mound still stands by the side of the road, just to the north of the bridge of Brodgar. Various finds, including some from the Iron Age, have come from this mound over the years. Geophysics has, once again, been carried out here recently and supports the suggestion that this mound covers a well-preserved broch site.

Further north, Iron Age evidence is lacking, though possible parallels between the earthworks at the Ring of Bookan and those at Mine Howe have been noted. Whether or not Bookan is Iron Age, the Iron Age farmers of the peninsula must have been very aware of the relict temples and numerous burial mounds that stood there. Some may still have worshipped at these sites, though they would have been an increasing minority. Others, no doubt, respected the ruins; some may have feared them. The structures at Barnhouse

and Ness of Brodgar, long since abandoned, may well have been plundered for good quality building stone.

At the bay of Skaill, Skara Brae was buried under sand, but there were Iron Age farmers in the vicinity. The sea is likely to have eroded further into the bay, though not to the extent that we see it today. The remains of an Iron Age settlement site can be seen eroding out of the dunes to the south of Skara Brae, and continuing erosion by the sea exposes occasional Iron Age burials. The farmers at Skaill lived in close proximity to the shore and they must have had to battle with the elements, just as their predecessors did at Skara Brae, but it is possible that the Iron Age economy at Skaill was based on the sea; the farmers would then have relied less on the products of the fields and well-being of their livestock, and would have been less vulnerable to the vagaries of climate and coastal erosion.

FIGURE 61.
Excavation work in the ditch surrounding Mine Howe.
ORKNEY ARCHAEOLOGICAL TRUST

CHAPTER NINE

Trade and Temptation:
The Picts, the Norse,
and the Coming of Christianity

Pictish Orkney

By the first century AD the name Orkney seems to have become established.
The name has Celtic roots and was used by Greek and Roman writers as well
as by later Irish historians. It suggests that the islands were inhabited by a tribe
who used the boar as their totem.[1] Wild boar are certainly recorded archaeologically from Orcadian sites, and boars crop up in more recent local folklore,
but it is also interesting to note that the boar was a common symbol of power
used by Pictish society.[2] The Celtic society of the late Iron Age in Scotland
seems to have coalesced into a new political configuration that is first clear in
the fourth century AD, but only starts to leave a recognisable archaeological
signal from the sixth century onwards: the Picts.[3]

Pictish Orkney was a society of farmers, developed from the Iron Age
communities which had gone before, which seems to have prospered. The first
written evidence appears in this period and lends colour to our interpretation
of life at this time, though the bulk of information still comes from archaeology. The early written texts were usually produced away from the Isles and
so only briefly refer to events in Orkney. Pictish society seems to have been
fairly rigidly stratified with craftsmen and farmers, as well as a local aristocracy
who were able to amass considerable wealth. Evidence is emerging of various
centres of power in the islands, including Birsay, in the west, and Mine Howe,
in the east (Figures 60 and 61). All gave allegiance to a local king.

Pictish dwellings

The Pictish inhabitants of Orkney lived in dispersed farms composed of
stone-built houses divided into several cellular rooms. Oats and bere barley
were the main crops, and cattle, sheep and pigs were kept; additionally, there
is evidence that activities like fishing began to grow in importance once again.
Individual farmsteads have been excavated at Buckquoy, in Birsay, and at
Skaill, in Deerness. Larger settlements comprising groups of houses did
exist, though there has been little excavation – several houses were revealed by

the excavations on the Brough of Birsay.[4] Elsewhere many of the broch sites were adapted. Defence was less important in this period and low Pictish-style dwellings were built amongst the old remains, using the old stonework.

Arts and crafts

Pictish Orkney is notable because it is the first time that we get a glimpse of the people themselves. Pictish art is renowned across Scotland and that from Orkney is no exception.[5] In addition to the commonly known carved symbol stones, the repertoire of Pictish art in Orkney has recently been enlarged with the addition of two small engravings on animal bone from a sand dune site in Burray. One is particularly engaging as it depicts a well-dressed man striding out (Figure 62).[6] He seems to be carrying a bag and is wearing a fringed tunic; the full details are only just being revealed. A fine symbol stone at Birsay is engraved with three figures, apparently a leader in fine dress and his two henchmen. Other Pictish art is more enigmatic and the symbols, though well known to the Picts, have yet to be deciphered; nevertheless, there is something uniquely personal about looking at these finely dressed figures with their weapons, drinking horns and other accoutrements.

The life of the Pictish family no doubt comprised hard work, but Pictish society was sophisticated. Archaeology has revealed considerable evidence for skilled metalworking in Pictish Orkney – some people were able to amass large quantities of fine goods, including jewellery, bowls and sword fittings. There is a remarkable uniformity in metal goods across Scotland in Pictish times, and this includes the motifs of decoration, many of which correspond to the motifs on the sculptured stones. Pictish craftsmen were highly skilled and they apparently worked to a rigid pattern book. A substantial metal workshop from Pictish times has been excavated at Mine Howe, showing that the site continued to be important for several centuries (Figures 60 and 61). Another metalworking centre existed on the Brough of Birsay, where much evidence for fine jewellery making has been discovered (Figure 63).[7] In general it seems that metalworking of this kind only took place in association with centres of power in the Pictish lands, suggesting that Pictish Orkney could support more than one leader with the wealth to accumulate resources and employ the craftsmen necessary, as well as the desire to acquire and display the finished goods.

Kingship and warriors

Metal goods are likely to have been commonplace only for the upper levels of Pictish society. The written references to the Picts suggest a highly stratified society, and it seems that Orkney had its own Pictish king who paid service to a king with a centralised power-base further south, such as King Bridei Mac Máelchý, near to Inverness. Not surprisingly, the Picts extended their influence through sea power as well as on land; it seems that King Bridei could command a substantial navy.

Pictish art does not just contain decorative motifs.[8] The meaning of many of the symbols may be hidden, but there is no mistaking others. Warriors and battle scenes appear on some of the carvings, especially further south in the Scottish mainland. The neighbourly aggression of the Iron Age may have disappeared, but warfare was a fundamental element of life in Pictish Scotland. Victories were something to be celebrated and recorded for posterity. Scholars today have identified some of the battle scenes on the southern Pictish stones with battles that are briefly mentioned in the few written sources from the time. Other stones celebrate the qualities of particular warriors. In the absence of engaged warfare they are depicted with their weapons and horses, riding out to the hunt or quaffing ale. Women, too, appear on the Pictish stones, but infrequently, and many of the qualities celebrated are (to our eyes) very masculine.

The arrival of Christianity

One of the main contributions of the Picts was the original establishment of Christianity in Orkney.[9] In the mid sixth century it was recorded that St Columba visited King Bridei near Inverness and, among other things, he begged safety for his hermits who were working in the north. He met with the Orcadian king, who had travelled south, visiting the court near Inverness. It is about this time that the first material goods relating to Christianity appear in the islands.

It seems that Christianity quickly took hold in Orkney, perhaps working through the existing secular hierarchy. One source suggests that a resident bishop was established at St Boniface in Papa Westray by the eighth century, though recent research suggests that this foundation may have Irish or Scandinavian, rather than Pictish, links. In addition, there are a number of churches with dedications to St Peter which have been interpreted by some archaeologists and historians as early.[10] Various isolated hermitage sites along the rocky coastlines have been recorded, such as the Castle of Burrian in Westray, and these may also have been used at this time. Even in the early Church a secular appreciation of fine things is reflected – an elaborately carved altar panel of stone from Flotta demonstrates that there was at least one church community able to make use of the Pictish skill in stone working.[11]

Pictish burial

Pictish burials in Orkney are few and far between but there arc hints as to burial practice in this period.[12] Burial in long cists, perhaps unmarked, may have taken place and short cists were also used. Even before the adoption of Christianity the evidence suggests that burial without grave goods was the norm. Some people have seen the fine Pictish symbol stones as grave markers, but this is not the case for all of them and as many graves did not have a lasting marker they remain elusive.

The Picts and the World Heritage Sites

Within the World Heritage area Pictish material is lacking. We can only speculate on what the Pictish inhabitants of Orkney thought of the great settings

FIGURE 62.
Pictish art provides our
first glimpse of our
ancestors themselves:
the wee Pictish man
from Burray.
ORKNEY MUSEUMS
AND HERITAGE

of standing stones and mounds of the ancestors as they made their way up the peninsula between the lochs. By the time of the Picts the stones were already nearly 3,000 years old and perhaps considered more alien to the Picts than Pictish remains themselves are to the world of today.

The Norse

Unlike Pictish society, Norse society in Orkney was based on incomers. The archaeological remains from the Pictish period suggest that defence was less

FIGURE 63.
The Brough of Birsay:
the remains in view are
those of the Viking
settlement, but
excavation showed
there had been earlier,
Pictish, activity here.
SIGURD TOWRIE

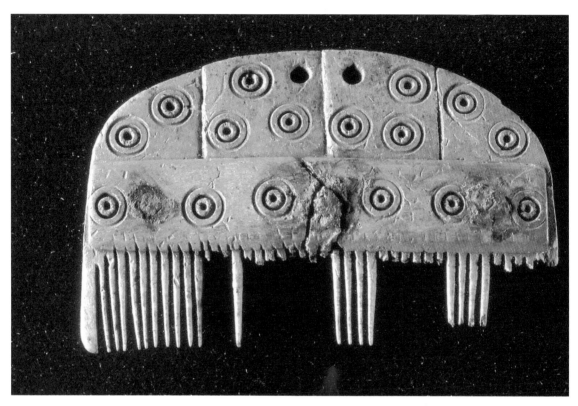

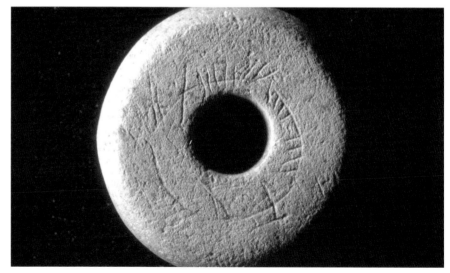

FIGURE 64.
A highly decorated bone comb (a) and a spindle whorl (b) with an inscription in ogham from the Pictish dwelling at Buckquoy. The inscription reads 'a blessing on the soul of L' and it is the earliest readable text from Orkney.

ORKNEY MUSEUMS AND HERITAGE

important, yet the written records show that from the late eighth century there was increasing pressure from overseas as the Vikings from western Norway became interested in northern Britain. Doubtless there was much to attract them. The Pictish aristocracy had amassed conspicuous riches, and both land and sea were fertile. By AD 900 there were Viking earls based in Orkney and their political influence extended south to the Scottish mainland and west to the Hebrides over the next couple of centuries. The Norse were a seafaring nation, and Orkney was ideally placed for them.[13]

Archaeology is rarely fine-tuned enough to see the precise moments of culture change and this is certainly true of the coming of the Norse. How did the existing Pictish population react? There is no sign of death and destruction on a large scale, no recorded skeletons or burial grounds. Scholars are divided in their interpretations of the nature of the changeover.[14] Whatever the mechanism by which it happened, the changes in lifestyle were all-embracing and rapid. Everyday life for the average Pict may not have been that different from the life of the Norse farmers, but some things must have had an impact. Christianity lost ground to new, popular, Viking gods. The Pictish language seems to have quickly fallen out of use as Norse influence spread. This is reflected sharply in the placenames of Orkney today – a network of Norse names exists across the islands with little hint of earlier times, indicating that a new system of local administration and taxation was soon established.[15] Landmarks were known by Norse nomenclature, surely a sign of new times if ever there was one, but the place names indicate other changes too. Even personal names began to reflect the new ways, as names of Scandinavian origin like Magnus and Sigurd became a familiar part of the Orkney scene.

Written evidence

Just as Pictish Orkney provided our first glimpse of the people of the past, Norse Orkney allows us to hear their voices and know their names. The Viking Sagas provide a great body of data, the precise truth of which is still a matter of academic debate. The sagas were put together to relate important events and family histories and they contain a wealth of information. They were first passed on by word of mouth, and then written down many years later, but they provide vibrant descriptions of both people and places. The main source of information relating to Orkney is the Orkneyinga Saga, which was compiled around the turn of the thirteenth century and recounts the history of the Norse Earldoms of the islands (Orkney and Shetland) and Caithness.[16] For the first time we not only have the archaeological sites, we also know the names of many of the people who walked the Orcadian landscape, and it is possible in some cases to tie the two together. Although archaeology remains an important source of information, with the Norse period Orkney moved into the realms of history.

Religion

Despite a religious presence in Pictish Orkney exemplified by the fine churches, Christianity seems to have waned with the coming of the Norsemen. There is no evidence for the survival of Christian communities from Pictish into later times, though knowledge of them seems to have persisted in the islands. Their sites were often selected by the Norse, who used names such as Papay (for example, Papa Westray), which may reflect the existence of a pre-Norse priest or priests, in order to give a sense of the past to their own island churches, newly created after their own conversion (Figure 65). Elsewhere it seems that the Norse gods held sway over much of the population. This is reflected in the popularity of pagan burials; Orkney contains more pagan graves from the Norse period than any other part of Scotland.[17] Although these tend to be early, dating from the mid ninth to mid tenth centuries AD, they add to the evidence for population disruption at this time and reinforce the idea that this was a period when Christian beliefs had fallen out of use.

It was not until the late tenth century that Christianity was once again introduced to the islands, with the conversion of Earl Sigurd and his followers. Earl Sigurd's conversion took place as a response to pressure from his rival Olaf Trygvesson.[18] It may well have been expedient, but he had certainly had exposure to Christian ways before this, as his mother and wife were both Christians. Academics still debate the stories of Sigurd's conversion, but nevertheless this event seems to have started the resurgence of Christianity in the Isles. By the mid eleventh century there was a boom in the building of churches and chapels throughout the islands, and this continued into the twelfth and thirteenth centuries with the foundation of parish churches.[19]

Settlement

Another of the changes that took place under the Norse involved the abandonment of old-fashioned Pictish-style houses and a fairly widespread adoption of a new type of house. Norse houses were long, rectangular in plan, and often spacious inside compared to the Pictish dwellings.[20] They had separate outbuildings. By now there were few trees in Orkney so they were built of stone and turf, with thatched roofs. Internally there were various fittings such as platforms and benches, and long central hearths. The Norse settlers lived in extended families, many of them in dispersed farmsteads, but larger communities began to grow up in one or two places. The Orkneyinga Saga notes the thriving market at Pierowall in Westray, where there was a sheltered harbour. By the end of the Norse period first Birsay and then Kirkwall had been established as larger settlements and centres of power (Figure 66).

The Norse economy was based on farming and environmental evidence from excavations such as that at Pool in Sanday,[21] Skaill in Deerness,[22] Birsay Bay[23] and Buckquoy[24] has provided much information regarding both crops and animals. Oats and barley were grown and the countryside was dotted with small horizontal mills used to process them. Flax, used to make linen, was introduced at this time. Cattle, sheep and pigs were kept, primarily for meat, together with horses and fowl. Both dogs and cats were present. The farmers were also successful fishermen; in some places, such as Quoygrew in Westray, there is evidence that fish were caught and processed in large quantities, to be exported to the growing population centres of northern Europe and Scandinavia.[25]

Local craftsmen and foreign skills

Not surprisingly for a society based on sea power, trade was vital to the Norse in Orkney. Exports from the islands included fish; imports included basics that were lacking, such as timber, as well as luxuries such as cloth and fine jewellery. Norse society was mobile; the menfolk tended to leave on long journeys over the summer months. Some were traders, some went to visit family and religious centres in the Norwegian homeland or further afield (even to Rome and the Holy Land), others went to fight and plunder. Orkney was well placed for this and the Norse in Orkney experienced a wider world than had most of their predecessors. Those who occupied the farmsteads uncovered by excavation will have had family around the northern seas, and tales and experiences of life elsewhere will have brightened many a dark night through the winter (Map 5).

By the Norse period, Orkney clearly had a longstanding tradition of local skills and this continued to develop. There was of course plenty of demand at home as the Norse Earls sought to show off their wealth and power. Fine imported raw materials were available and finished goods brought in from overseas must have stimulated local traditions. Over the years, archaeology has revealed many fine objects from Norse Orkney. They come from a variety of settings, including settlement sites, burials and hoards, and include jewellery, weaponry and household objects.

FIGURE 65.
The Norse church at Orphir.
RAYMOND PARKS

FIGURE 66.
Remains of the settlement outside the Orphir Kirk.
RAYMOND PARKS

MAP 5.
Orkney lay at the heart of things for the sea-faring Norsemen.
KENNY SWINNEY

Ireland

Scotland

ORKNEY

Shetland

Norway

Churchmen and builders

In addition to the earlier chapels, the later Norse period saw the establishment of the parish system in the islands, and the foundation of many parish churches took place at this time.[26]

The culmination of Norse church building in Orkney has, however, to be the magnificent Cathedral of St Magnus, which still dominates religious life in the islands nearly 1,000 years after it was constructed. In 1137 Earl Rognvald founded the cathedral, and work started to build a fitting church in Kirkwall to celebrate both the Earl's power and the considerable reputation of his uncle, St Magnus (himself a former Earl, who had been murdered in Orkney at the age of 35 in 1115). Saints at this time were highly significant and, as a local saint, St Magnus was very much a part of the Norse community. The cathedral was designed to promote and preserve the reputation of Magnus and his relics, and also led to Rognvald gaining the power and respect which later led to his canonization as a second warrior saint for Orkney (Figure 67).

The cathedral was an ambitious project;[27] it involved masons who had worked on some of the finest cathedrals further south, such as Durham and Dunfermline, together with many different craftsmen brought in to work on the interior fittings.[28] The population of Kirkwall shot up, as did its prosperity, with people needing lodgings, food and other services. Kirkwall became the focus of the newly created diocese of Orkney and Shetland, and the cathedral, as the reliquary of St Magnus, represented the final station on his pilgrimage route. The scene was set for Kirkwall to dominate the economic and cultural life of the islands.[29]

Building work in the islands was not confined to religious foundations. In the mid twelfth century, perhaps during the time of Bishop William, work started on the Bishop's Palace, a fine residence which was to be part of the cathedral complex in Kirkwall. The Bishop's Palace is a remarkable building, for though it reflects the high status architecture of Norway at the time, it has been adapted to meet the needs and designs of Orkney. It provides an indication of the wealth and power of the late Norse church and went on to influence local architecture, as wealthy Orcadians sought to create their own buildings in similar style. The remains of hall-houses built in this style have been found at Westness in Rousay, Tuquoy in Westray, and Skaill in Deerness, to name but a few. Together these wealthy dwellings reflect the diverse influences and wealth of the islands in the twelfth and thirteenth centuries.

Fighting and politics

Warfare and fighting were integral to Norse society. If the Norse did not have their own battles to fight they often joined others. Politics played an important part in this, particularly since Orkney was at the heart of a complex web of opposing factions:[30] not only was there the dual nature of the Earldoms of Orkney and Caithness, which were often split between antagonistic parts of the family; there were the opposing demands of the Norwegian and Scottish crowns, both vying for influence in Orkney; and allegiances with other political figures such as that which led to the presence of Orkney men at the Battle of Clontarf in Ireland in 1014. Throughout the thirteenth century the Scottish crown was able to exert increasing influence in the north and this included affairs in Orkney, especially after the death of the last Norse Earl, Earl John, in Thurso in 1231.

Burial

Those who came home and died in Orkney were laid to rest in a variety of ways.[31] Orkney contains a rich heritage of pagan Norse burials, many of which are quite elaborate. There were cemeteries, such as those at Pierowall in Westray and Westness in Rousay, but some were buried in isolation. Mounds were erected over some graves, some bodies were inserted into existing mounds and some were laid to rest in flat graves. Both stone-built cists as well as unlined pits were used and some burials, both men and women, have rich and elaborate grave goods. At least one family was laid to rest in a boat, at Scar in Sanday, together with fine household objects as well as weapons and jewellery.[32]

With the coming of Christianity people went about burial in very different ways. Grave goods were abandoned and simple graves were laid out, nearly always in the vicinity of a church. Many graves from this period are unmarked today, though possible evidence for simple markers may be seen in the regularity of the neat rows of burials at sites such as Tammaskirk in Rendall. At other cemeteries, such as the twelfth-century Bu of Cairston outside Stromness, the archaeologists found slots which may have been sockets for markers. In addition, a few, later, graves were given a distinctive stone marker – a long low stone laid over the length of the burial and designed to represent the shingle roof of a building – known as a hogback. Hogbacks occur across Scotland and there are four in Orkney, two of which may be seen in the Orkney Museum in Kirkwall.

The Norse in the World Heritage Area

Norse literature and mythology reflects a deep sense of the passage of time and the importance of the ancestors. How did the Norse peoples of Orkney react to the standing stones that were already nearly 4,000 years old? They certainly visited them, and in a touch that is resonant even today, left their mark in the form of graffiti carved on to various stones. The biggest collection of graffiti is that inside Maeshowe (Figure 68); other small runic inscriptions include that on one of the stones at the Ring of Brodgar, two isolated field finds, and one in the nearby Neolithic tomb at Unstan. The graffiti from the World Heritage area is considered particularly important by those who study the Norse, which is a sobering thought when we consider how much modern graffiti is left for posterity!

Maeshowe seems to have been particularly significant to the Norse. Archaeologists have suggested that it was adapted and used for the burial of a wealthy chieftain in the ninth century. Whether or not this took place, the

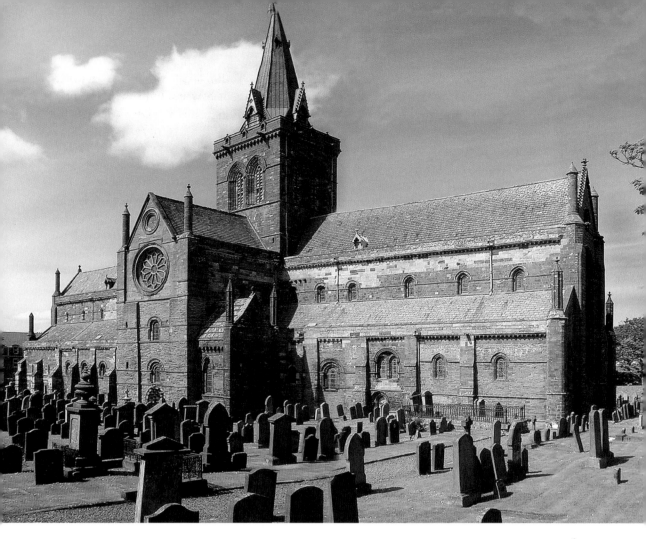

FIGURE 67.
St Magnus Cathedral,
Kirkwall.
RAYMOND PARKS

tomb was entered by Norsemen on several occasions and it seems to have both attracted and repelled those who explored it. The importance of Maeshowe at this time is reflected in the fact that the tomb today contains one of the greatest collections of runic graffiti in existence. Not surprisingly, the runes tell a variety of stories.[33] On one occasion a group of warriors was forced into the tomb to seek shelter from a great storm. The men were inside for a couple of days, in which period they record that two of their number went mad. Other messages are more mundane, boasting of great prowess as rune carvers or with the axe: 'Arnfithr, son of Stein, carved these runes'. The beauty and merits of various ladies are recorded, and there is mention of a great treasure that was removed from the tomb: '... treasure was carried off in three nights ...'. As the Neolithic builders of Maeshowe would not have known of gold, this has been cited as evidence for later burials at Maeshowe, but it may also have been wishful thinking or twelfth-century 'urban legend'.

Maeshowe was prominent in the landscape of Norse Orkney, and it clearly played a prominent role for the communities around it. So, too, must have the standing stones. The Stones of Stenness gave their name to the largest township in the parish, and later became incorporated as the name for the parish itself. In addition, it may be no coincidence that a tall standing stone which stood in the field to the north of the Stones of Stenness until the early nineteenth century was known by a name with Norse connotations: the Stone of Odin. Archaeological excavations have confirmed the Neolithic origin of the Stone of Odin,[34] but up to its destruction it was used in many ways, particularly for the confirmation of contracts, often marriages. The Stone of Odin was perforated by a hole and nineteenth-century tradition records that it would be visited by lovers who pledged their troth by holding hands through the hole.[35] The 'oath of Odin' was very seriously regarded and the hole must have been sizeable because another ritual involved the passing of a newborn baby through it in order to ensure a healthy life.

Further north along the Brodgar peninsula, eighteenth-century records refer to the finding of nine silver arm-rings in one of the mounds near to the Ring of Brodgar. The context in which they were originally hidden remains unknown: rather than being part of a burial it is possible that they were part of a hoard. Norse Orkney held its own uncertainties and a number of deliberately hidden metal hoards have been found. The owner of this one was perhaps hoping that the power of the spirits who still resided in and around the stones and burial mounds might help to protect their wealth.

Another well-known hoard comes from the Bay of Skaill, on the shores of which lay Skara Brae. Skara Brae itself was long abandoned and must have been ruinous and hidden, but Skaill is a Norse name suggesting that a hall or dwelling lay here,[36] and this is not the only strand of evidence suggesting Norse activity near by.[37] Several possible Norse burials have been recorded, including a cemetery site discovered during work on the present car park at Skaill House. It has been suggested that the two skeletons recovered from House 7 during

FIGURE 68.
Viking graffiti in
Maeshowe.
SIGURD TOWRIE

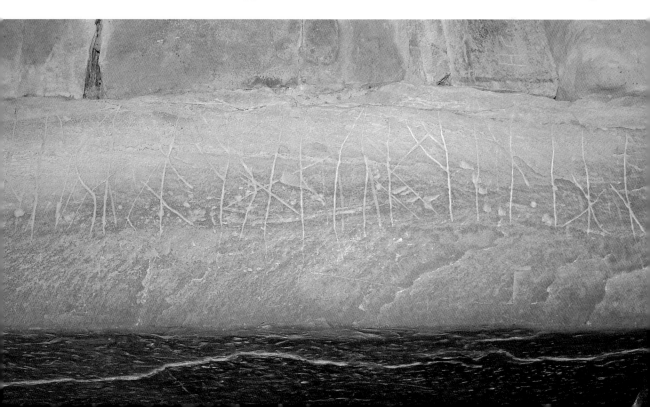

the 1930 excavations at Skara Brae may date to this time, and there are further indications of a chapel site adjacent to the car park at the Heritage Centre.

The Skaill hoard was recovered in 1858, apparently in a mound near the present church.[38] It is one of the largest Viking hoards from Scotland. It comprises almost 7 kg of silver and includes jewellery, ingots and coins. There may have been an early kirk here and, if so, there is likely to have been a high-status settlement in the area. In 2004 David Griffiths began excavations on the mound, now known as the Castle of Snusgar, to investigate the probable location of the hoard. His work has only just started, though it has already yielded Norse artefacts such as bone combs.[39]

This all adds weight to the argument for a Norse settlement of some status at Skaill, and it is interesting that the township here was to give its name to the parish; another indication of the importance of the area in the twelfth and thirteenth centuries.

CHAPTER TEN

Farmland, Famine and Visitors: Historic Orkney into the Twentieth Century

With the twelfth century we move into the late medieval period and the nature of information relating to the past changes as documentary evidence becomes more commonplace. Archaeology continues to play an important role, particularly relating to everyday life, but as records relating to a wealth of material including names, treaties and local court cases become widespread so we move into the world of history. This means that not only do we need to understand the way of life as reflected in past material culture and the traces that people have left on the land, we also need to understand the political forces that acted to shape the lives of the inhabitants of Orkney. This was a complex period that saw many changes, starting with the transfer of allegiance to Scotland and the general reduction in Norse ways across the islands,[1] and ending with a truly international dimension as Orkney played a key role in two world wars. This chapter provides a potted background to these political and historical events and looks at the way they have shaped the sites and monuments from the period that occur across the island landscape (and seascape).

Political transfer to Scotland

The process of 'Scottification' in Orkney[2] was slow and involved gradual change in the cultural and economic life of the islands throughout the twelfth and thirteenth centuries.[3] Political change was not to come until later. In 1231 Earl John, the last of the Scandinavian earls of Orkney, was murdered in Thurso. This marked the end of an era and the earldom passed to his kinsmen, the Earls of Angus. Although the Earls of Angus were of Scottish descent, at first their political allegiance stayed with the Norwegian kings. Over time, nevertheless, the influence of Orkney's powerful southern neighbour was increasingly felt. The earldom passed through several Scottish houses and each successive earl attracted various members of his family and others north to seek wealth and stability in the islands. This was not always advantageous for the local people, as their new overlords sought to raise taxes and influence local trade and land ownership, but it brought about a gradual increase in Scottish aristocracy and influence in Orkney. Finally, in 1468, Orkney was passed to the Scottish Crown.[4]

The influence of the Scandinavian Crown had waned steadily over these 200 years, partly due to events at home in Norway and Denmark, so the transfer of power probably had little impact on the daily lives of most Orcadians. The manner of transfer, however, was notable in that Orkney was mortgaged by the Danish (and Norwegian) king in lieu of paying out a dowry upon the marriage of his daughter Margaret to James III of Scotland. Orkney at the time was worth 50,000 florins of the Rhine and the mortgage was never paid off, or annulled, a fact that resurfaces from time to time when policies made in the south irritate the island population.

Sinclairs and Stewarts

The Earls of Orkney at the time of transfer were the Sinclairs. Despite their political allegiance to Scandinavia, they were a Scottish family from Roslin near Edinburgh, though the first Sinclair earl, Earl Henry, spent much time in Orkney and was keen to develop his lands there. Earl Henry built a strong castle in Kirkwall, sadly long gone except as a street name. With the transfer to Scotland the Sinclairs lost their titles and for most of the next century political power was managed through the Scottish Crown. The Sinclairs were a powerful and large family, however, with branches in Caithness as well as Orkney, and needless to say there was constant in-fighting between factions. In 1529 strife within the Sinclair family came to the fore with the last battle on Orkney soil, the Battle of Summerdale, which took place at the boundary between Orphir and Stenness between two Sinclair cousins, leading armies of Caithness men against Orcadians.[5] The Caithness men were apparently routed, but the generally disruptive situation in the north led to King James V himself making a visit.

In 1565 the earldom was granted by Mary Queen of Scots to her half-brother Robert Stewart and Orkney moved into a period known as that of the Stewart Earls.[6] Earl Robert, his son Patrick and grandson Robert held sway in the islands for fifty years. Even today these years are remembered as a time of great difficulty and hardship. The Stewarts were ambitious and extravagant.[7] They appropriated land across the islands and levied high rents and taxes. Towards the end of the sixteenth century Earl Robert started work on a fine palace at Birsay and in the early seventeenth century Earl Patrick built a magnificent palace in Kirkwall (Figure 69). Both are ruined today and are noted as much for the forced labour of the islanders that contributed to their construction as for the elegance of their architecture and fittings. The Stewarts did not enjoy a long dominion, however. Earl Patrick and his son Robert were both executed in Edinburgh in 1615.

FIGURE 69.
The Earl's Palace, Kirkwall.
RAYMOND PARKS

Cromwell

The Stewarts were the last great earls to create a powerbase in Orkney. The mid seventeenth century saw events take a new turn, when a Cromwellian garrison was sent from the south and occupied Kirkwall. St Magnus Cathedral was used as stabling, but not everyone was impressed by the grandeur of their surroundings and there are some colourful descriptions of Orkney attributed to the incoming soldiers: 'Their schooles of learning are in every house, and their first lesson is to hunt the louse'.[8] After this Orkney moved more into the mainstream of Scottish events as those who held power here also had interests elsewhere.

Social life

With the end of the Norse period, Orkney emerged from prehistory into history and everyday life becomes more recognisable for those of us in the early twenty-first century, though there were obvious differences. Initially the old Norse language, Norn, was still spoken.[9] Scandinavian customs became less common, however, as Scottish laws and taxes were gradually introduced. The Scottish population in the islands had been growing slowly and from now on it steadily increased. One big change was the adoption of the Scottish custom of using surnames. Up to that time the Norse patronymic system of naming children after their father was followed. Life for the people of Orkney still revolved around farming, fishing and trade. Houses were simple and furnishings were often basic. The years from the fourteenth century onwards saw considerable ups and downs in island life.[10]

Famine and plague

Fourteenth-century Europe experienced a deterioration in climate which had a serious adverse impact on farming, and Orkney did not escape its effects. To make things worse, in 1349 Orkney – like the rest of Europe – was hit by the plague with a devastating effect on population, and thus on the workforce. By the mid fifteenth century the population of the islands had declined to such a level that many farmsteads were standing empty.[11] Shifts of power overseas had affected trade badly and life cannot have been easy for the people of the islands. The heavy taxation of the Stewart Earls in the following centuries came at a bad time.

The seventeenth century saw further poor weather and famine continued to strike, combined with a return of the plague in 1629.[12] Some 4,000 people are estimated to have died in this century. The general stagnation of agriculture meant that the land systems across Orkney (as elsewhere in the Highlands and across Scotland) were run on the medieval system of run rig, a communal land division that limited crops and yields. Life for the farmers of Orkney was not to improve until the early eighteenth century.

Eighteenth- and nineteenth-century improvements

In contrast to the preceding centuries, eighteenth-century Orkney saw various developments that improved island life considerably. Agricultural improvements were a high priority for the landowners, but brought mixed success.[13] New crops (potatoes) were introduced, some enclosure took place, and land was divided on a different system, known as planking. However, farmers often managed to subdivide their lands, thus reducing the impact of the new system. Other improvements were more ambitious, such as the construction of a great cattle farm in South Ronaldsay.

Orkney also had local resources that came to the fore in these years. The kelp industry was the first, exploiting the seaweed that abounded along the shore.[14] Kelp could be burnt and exported as a glassy slag; its high alkali content meant that it was in great demand for industries such as glass and soap further south. The kelp industry spread quickly through the islands and employed about 3,000 islanders at its peak, but it was a short-lived boom and by 1830 kelp prices had plummeted as other sources and artificial substitutes were developed. The industry collapsed, but the coasts of Orkney today are littered with small round kilns sunk into the turf and long low walls on which the tangles were dried before burning. These provide a mute testament to the activity that once took place.

While the kelp industry was flourishing others found work in the production of local linen and straw goods. Both relied on imported materials and were carried out at home. Flax from the Baltic was turned into fine linen, while imported straw was used for goods such as bonnets. By the mid nineteenth century, however, the linen industry had disappeared as mechanisation further south provided cheap competition, and straw work was on the decline,[15] though a strong craft-tradition of island straw work has survived in Orkney to the present day.

Although these industries were controlled by the landowners, they did impact on life for everyone. Plenty of work kept island populations high, and both linen and straw brought some financial independence to the women. The landowners were able to build fine houses in Kirkwall and elsewhere,[16] and import the necessities of life from the south. Although little enough wealth trickled down to the workers, it did mean that they could afford luxuries, such as tea and coffee, which were not easily available elsewhere.

A life at sea

There was work in the islands, but many men still opted for a life at sea. Developments in boats and navigation in the eighteenth century meant that longer trips became the norm. Fishing had obviously always been of local importance but it was given new significance at this time with the development of commercial fishing. This was to bloom in the nineteenth century with the arrival of the herring fleet, which brought many hundreds of extra workers into the islands for the short herring season and led to the development of industrial scale communities in islands such as Stronsay and Burray.[17] Whaling, too, provided steady, if more dangerous, employment and many men left to join the fleets that supplied the markets with whalebone and blubber.

Orkney was strategically well placed for the sailing ships that crossed the Atlantic and many came in to Stromness for a reliable source of fresh water. Not surprisingly, they would use this as an opportunity to pick up crews and Orkneymen were known for their relevant skills. This included not only seamen: carpenters, blacksmiths, tailors and clerks were all needed, especially with the development of trading companies such as the Hudson's Bay

FIGURE 70.
Kirbuster farmstead
dates back at least to
the early eighteenth
century.
RAYMOND PARKS

Company, which valued the Orkneymen for their hardy survival skills in the northern lands.[18]

Tourists

In addition to the resident population of the islands another force was coming to the fore: visitors. Although tourism did not really take off until the nineteenth century, with improved transport and the popularisation of Scotland, Orkney was a popular destination for many early travellers, and several published illustrated accounts of their visits.[19] These provide a fascinating glimpse of the islands and it is interesting to see that the archaeological sites attracted tourists from early on.

Prominent visitors such as Sir Walter Scott played an important role in promoting Orkney and from the nineteenth century onwards tourism started to influence the local economy. This increased dramatically throughout the twentieth century,[20] at the end of which Orkney was one of the most visited cruise destinations in Britain, not to mention visitors who arrive by other transport.

In the twenty-first century archaeology has come to play an increasing role in attracting visitors, together with the birds, flora, and the potential for recreational diving. The spin-off from tourism has meant a flourishing local economy with little unemployment (though many jobs are poorly paid and seasonal). The local craft industry has also benefited from the large numbers of visitors keen to take away a high quality souvenir.

The twentieth-century economy: wartime and peace

In addition to the tourists, the twentieth century saw its own great influx of personnel during the two World Wars. Orkney occupied a key strategic position in both wars; in the First World War about 100,000 people were sent here. Many were billeted on board the navy ships, but there were also land forces and the economic repercussions across the islands were widespread. Not only did everyone have to be fed and looked after, but the island infrastructure had to be able to cope with them; roads were improved and local services increased.

The wartime attractions of Orkney came about because of its location.

Scapa Flow was of great strategic importance as it was the ideal place from which to control the north Atlantic.[21] It offered a sheltered harbour that was large enough to base the Great Fleet in 1914–18. This may have been a safe base, but wartime Orkney was not without its tragedies, as ships ventured out to play their part. In 1916 the HMS *Hampshire* set sail from Lyness on Hoy, bound for Murmansk in Russia; on board was the supreme commander of the British forces, Field Marshall Earl Kitchener of Khartoum. It was a stormy night and the ship's course was altered at the last minute. As she sailed past the cliffs of Marwick Head on the western coast of the Orkney Mainland she struck a mine and sank. Only twelve crew members survived, and Kitchener himself was lost. In 1917 there was disaster with the loss of HMS *Vanguard* which blew up at her moorings due to an internal explosion; there were only two survivors and over 1,000 dead.

At the end of the war the German High Seas Fleet was brought to Orkney to be interned while the allies decided its fate. 4,000 crew members were kept on to maintain the 74 ships. In the end the fate of the fleet was taken out of allied hands. After six months of uncertainty the German Admiral issued coded orders to scuttle the ships; within five hours most lay at the bottom of

FIGURE 71.
Relics along the shore
at Stromness bear mute
testament to a maritime
past.
RAYMOND PARKS

the Flow, with the loss of nine German crew. In the years leading up to the Second World War many of these boats were salvaged, but seven still lie on the sea bed and provide an additional attraction to tourists. Diving has become another mainstay of the local economy.

The strategic importance of Scapa Flow was extended in the First World War with the arrival of the first war planes. There were small air stations on land and trials included the landing of planes on the ships; the first successful landing on a moving aircraft carrier took place in the Flow towards the end of the war on HMS *Furious*, and in 1918 she was used for the first carrier-based strike, which involved seven Sopwith Camels.[22]

By the time of the Second World War the air force was an important part of the garrison and four airfields were built, as well as two dummy air bases.[23] Scapa Flow continued to house the fleet, but late in 1939 a German U-boat penetrated the defences and entered the Flow. It took two rounds of torpedo fire but she successfully struck the HMS *Royal Oak*, which lay at anchor at the mouth of Scapa Bay. The *Royal Oak* sank in less than fifteen minutes and over 800 of the crew of 1,400 were drowned. Churchill came north to inspect the defences of the flow and ordered the construction of barriers to block access between the chain of islands that guarded the eastern side of the Flow. Work on the barriers resulted in the creation of an industrial landscape as huge concrete blocks were cast and carried out into the channels to be sunk.

Much of the workforce comprised prisoners, many of them Italians captured in north Africa, and a lasting, if unexpected, monument was left behind in the form of the Italian Chapel on Lambholm. Once the heart of a prison camp and the centre of barrier engineering, this is now a peaceful spot. The chapel itself is housed in a corrugated iron Nissan hut, but the unpromising exterior gives way to an ornate interior where, with paint and the skilful use of any materials they could lay their hands on, the prisoners, under the direction of Domenico Chiochetti, were able to create the impression of a traditional church. The chapel is very much in use today for concerts and recitals as well as the occasional service, and it has become a place of pilgrimage for people from around the world.

Although they were of tremendous defensive significance when first built, the Churchill barriers are still in use. Today they are crossed by the main road between the south isles and they have come to play a vital economic role. Rather than acting as a barrier they serve to join the communities of the islands.

The garrison of the Second World War left another memorial of its stay. It seems that conditions for visiting troops in Orkney had not improved since the time of Cromwell and there is another poem which recites the local charms:

> This bloody town's a bloody cuss,
> No bloody trains, no bloody bus,

And no one cares for bloody us
In bloody Orkney.
The bloody roads are bloody bad,
The bloody folks are bloody mad,
They'd make the brightest bloody sad,
In bloody Orkney.[24]
All bloody clouds, and bloody rains,
No bloody kerbs, no bloody drains,
The Council's got no bloody brains,
In bloody Orkney.[25]

The twentieth century provided its own economic booms, from the short-lived Orkney egg industry and the development of butter and cheese markets, to the arrival of the oil industry in the 1970s. By the end of the century this was joined by fish-farming and an upturn in local crafts and quality foods. These were often initially aimed at the local tourist market but many have quickly developed outlets further south. The development of information technology has served to boost the island economy further; not only has it made it more easy for people to access information about Orkney from around the world, but it has also facilitated those who wished to relocate and work in a more rural environment.

Religion

Since the end of the Norse period Christianity has been established in the islands. Throughout recent centuries burial has taken place according to

FIGURE 72.
Tank training at the Ring of Brodgar gives an idea of how attitudes to the monuments have changed.
IWMH 10589

131

Christian practice and the number of church and chapel foundations across Orkney show that religion has remained an important aspect of everyday life. The Reformation in the mid sixteenth century brought change as it did elsewhere, but Orkney seems to have escaped the worst of the disruption that sometimes took place. Most of the early religious houses across the islands seem to have gone out of use long before this. St Magnus Cathedral was not targeted for damage; interestingly it has always belonged to the burgh of Kirkwall, having been transferred from the Royal estate in 1468 by James III when the islands were handed over to Scotland. St Magnus is unique in belonging to the community it serves and it is still a very active place of worship.[26]

There are, however, hints that the early Norse ways have not been completely forgotten, though they are slowly dying out as we move into the twenty-first century. Odin figures strongly in Orkney tradition and though there is likely to have been some embellishment of old ways down the years, especially from the nineteenth-century romantics, it is also possible to see that the force of pre-Christian beliefs and customs was very much a part of life in recent years.[27] The Odin Oath, for example, was a powerful agreement sealed at the Odin Stone until the stone's destruction in 1814 (Figure 73). Not surprisingly, fire also played an important role in local celebrations, but while some traditions have died out, such as the Johnsmas or midsummer bonfires, others, such as the midwinter bonfires, have been adapted into modern life with the use of fireworks at New Year.

FIGURE 73.
A nineteenth-century depiction of the Odin Stone.
COURTESY OF THE ORKNEY LIBRARY AND ARCHIVE PHOTOGRAPHIC LIBRARY

The World Heritage Sites in historic times

The Ness of Brodgar was still visited up to the late medieval period for sacred and celebratory reasons, though those who went there can have had no idea of the original purposes of the monument builders. Odin's Stone was a popular and important place to plight marriages and other oaths up to the nineteenth century, when, as mentioned above, it was removed.

Just to the north of the Ring of Brodgar runs the Dyke of Sean, an earthwork which extends from loch to loch. It is possible that the Dyke was originally Bronze Age in date, but other sources suggest it may be medieval. At the south end of the peninsula lies the parish church of Stenness, which is likely to go back to pre-Reformation times and possibly earlier. The present building is the latest of three and though precise information about the earlier buildings is lacking it is clear that this has been an important Christian site for centuries. The parish of Stenness extends some distance to the south, west and east, and it is interesting that the church founders chose to build so close to the ancient stone settings (which finally gave their name to the parish). One cannot help but feel that the area was still important to them.[28] Interestingly, there are suggestions that there may once have been a high status mansion house here, to the south-east of the kirkyard. There is nothing visible today, but tradition tells of the Palace of Stenness, from the upper storey of which it was possible to see the ships sailing into Stromness.[29]

In the eighteenth century the traditional run-rig system of land division continued in the parish of Stenness. Recent geophysical survey has confirmed the existence of traces of agriculture in the area of the World Heritage sites. Agricultural concerns became increasingly dominant and in 1815 the tenant farmer demolished two of the surviving stones at the Stones of Stenness. He was stopped while something of the monument survived, but the extant stones along the peninsula have gradually been removed over the years so that only a fragment of the original stone settings remains. Nineteenth- and early twentieth-century concerns with the monuments were not all negative, however. In 1908 three stones were set up into a 'dolmen' arrangement at the centre of the Stones of Stenness. Although this was somewhat controversial and no longer exists, excavation in 1973 suggested that it did reflect the original arrangement of the stones.[30] Elsewhere, many fallen stones were re-erected in the early twentieth century when the sites were taken into state care.

The Ring of Brodgar was first mentioned in 1529 by Jo Ben,[31] a visitor to the islands, and the Stones of Stenness was recorded in 1700. Maeshowe, as we have seen, was broken into by the Vikings, and the first academic publication of this site goes back to James Farrer in 1862.[32] Skara Brae came to light in 1850. Through recent centuries the monuments have all attracted considerable attention, some of it academic and antiquarian (Chapter Eleven) and some relating to wider cultural interests such as art and literature.

Artistic depictions of the standing stones and Maeshowe abound. From the eighteenth century onwards they have been a popular subject of inspiration and the early depictions are very useful today in providing a good idea of the state of the monuments at different times. Not surprisingly, they still provide fertile ground for artists of various traditions. Historically, Skara Brae has figured less in art, partly because of its relatively recent discovery and partly because of the very different nature of the site, though it is a popular subject today.

Orkney folklore abounds with stories that feature the stones and other sites and this tradition has been carried through to modern literature. Some authors, such as George Mackay Brown, have written modern versions of the old stories, itself an important step to ensure that they are not lost in modern times. Others have featured the monuments in new stories. Literature featuring the sites includes both children's tales, such as the popular *Boy with the Bronze Axe* by Kathleen Fidler, and adult stories, like *Early in Orcadia* by Naomi Mitchison.

Many archaeological sites in Orkney have had an impact on the cultural life of the islands but the impact of the World Heritage Sites, perhaps because of their own inherent quality, has been particularly vibrant. Whether as inspiration for tunes, the subjects of poetry, the covers of compact discs and books, or material for exhibitions, the archaeological sites permeate life in Orkney.

It is also worth noting how this influence has spread. The importance of tourism to the Orkney economy in the twentieth century is well recorded. Many tourists were attracted to Orkney because of the archaeology and they have increased in number through the twentieth century. A survey in 2000 suggests that about 60 per cent of tourists in Orkney were attracted here because of the sites, of which the World Heritage Sites are the best known. Two-thirds of the visitors had heard of Skara Brae before their visit while only half had heard of Highland Park distillery![33]

At the start of the twenty-first century the cultural and economic impact of Skara Brae and the sites of the Ness of Brodgar in Orkney must be comparable, if different, to their impact some 5,000 years ago, when they were newly built. Modern society places great store by its roots and these sites provide tangible connections that can still be visited in a way that has disappeared at the great, managed sites of the south of England such as Stonehenge. The visitor to Stonehenge today is kept away from the monument, treads a carefully built path, and has to share the experience with thousands of other people. Although the sites of Orkney are carefully monitored, and Skara Brae receives some 60,000 visitors a year, they still provide a relatively untamed experience. In a sense, for some people the experience of visiting them must differ little to that of our Neolithic ancestors 5,000 years ago. Each interprets the monuments in terms of their own culture and needs. For others it is a more basic, economic devotion – those who come to visit the sites help to keep Orkney, as a thriving community, alive.

CHAPTER ELEVEN

Antiquarians and Archaeologists

Antiquarians and their modern counterparts, archaeologists, have been very influential in the development of Orkney's archaeological sites. At the same time, the archaeological sites of Orkney have played a key role in the development of archaeological theory and practice, not only in Scotland but further afield.[1] The quality of the remains has undoubtedly helped; it attracted people to Orkney, and provided them with well-preserved sites and plenty of information. There is, as we have seen, no shortage of work on the archaeological sites of Orkney, yet despite this they still provide fruitful ground for further research. This means that in the early twenty-first century Orkney is still the focus for many research projects; many archaeologists are visitors but there is also a thriving, and increasing, local population of archaeologists.

Early references to the antiquities of Orkney

The first written reference to the antiquities of Orkney dates back to the sixteenth century, although it was first published in 1805, by the Reverend Barry, in his *History of Orkney*.[2] It concerns an enigmatic Latin manuscript, *Descriptio Insularum Orchadiarum*, apparently written by one Jo Ben in 1529. Ben describes a tomb, probably Maeshowe, which contained the bones of a man together with coins, and he also mentions a nearby circle of standing stones. Although Ben's description is brief and perhaps exaggerated (he describes the man as being 14 feet tall), it is interesting that the World Heritage Sites were already noteworthy.

Interest in the stones and mounds of Orkney grew through the following centuries, but it suffered from a lack of expertise and focus. There was no shortage of people ready to write about the sites and their possible interpretation, but their explanations were often fanciful and their sources vague. In 1693, for example, the Reverend Wallace[3] equated the Ring of Brodgar and the Stones of Stenness with the worship of the sun (at the former) and the moon (at the latter), but it is unclear whether he was reporting local tradition or current academic theory. Most authorities considered the circles to represent ancient temples, but it is difficult to know how much each was relying upon the account of his predecessors.

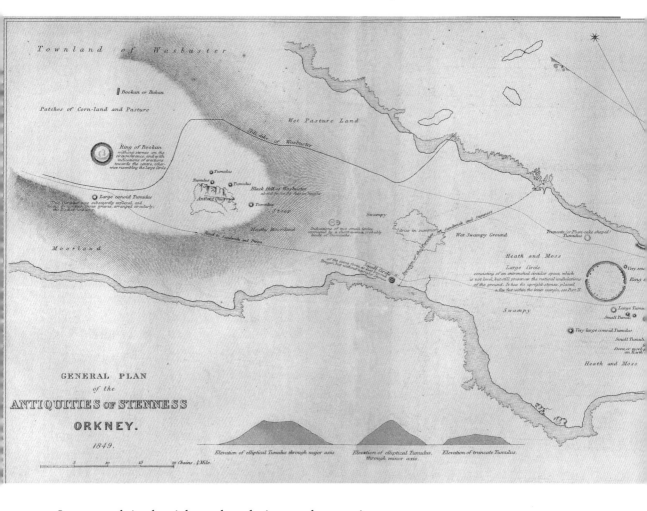

Survey work in the eighteenth and nineteenth centuries

Towards the end of the eighteenth century the approach of those interested in the sites began to change, in line with developments in scientific observation and reasoning which made it easier for people to gather and analyse factual data relating to the sites, such as measurements. In 1772 Orkney was visited by Sir Joseph Banks on his way to Iceland. Banks was leading a scientific expedition and his ship, the *Sir Lawrence*, spent several days in Stromness. Banks' team took advantage of their stay to explore several mounds around the bay of Skaill, and they carried out both excavation and survey. Although the excavations left a lot to be desired by modern standards, the surveys, undertaken by Frederick Walden, surveyor with the expedition, still provide an important record of the state of the sites at the time. Seventeen years later further survey work was carried out by Sir John Stanley, who also had a clear eye for detail.

Another important survey project took place in 1850 when the Royal Navy survey ship *Woodlark* called in to Stromness. The commander, Captain F. W. L. Thomas, took the opportunity to investigate various local antiquities.

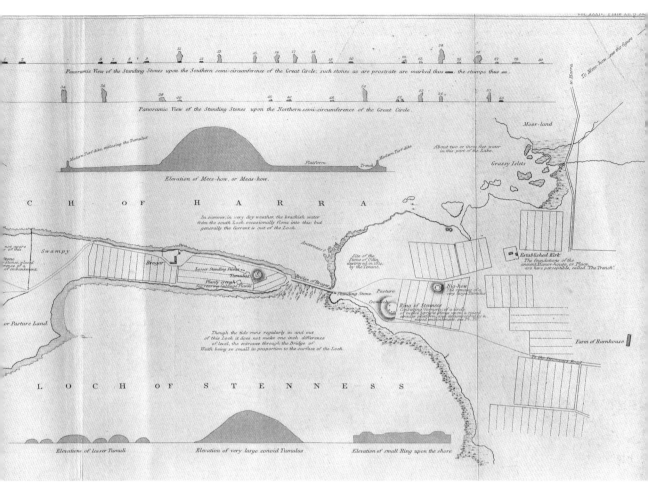

Panoramic View of the Standing Stones upon the Southern semi-circumference of the Great Circle; such stones as are prostrate are marked thus ▬ the stumps thus ▬

Panoramic View of the Standing Stones upon the Northern semi-circumference of the Great Circle.

Elevation of Mees-how, or Meas-how.

Elevations of lesser Tumuli   Elevation of very large conoid Tumulus   Elevation of small Ring upon the shore

FIGURE 74.
Thomas' survey of the
Brodgar peninsula
provides detail that is
still of use today.

COURTESY OF THE
ORKNEY LIBRARY AND
ARCHIVE
PHOTOGRAPHIC
LIBRARY

Thomas' work is interesting because he concentrated not only on the larger, well-known, sites, but also on more minor monuments. Thomas' work included a topographic survey of the Ness of Brodgar and he accompanied this with detailed descriptions which still form an important record today (Figures 74 and 75).[4] He also undertook some excavation, though excavation standards at the time mean that this work is less helpful to modern archaeologists. Thomas was concerned with issues of preservation and the disposal of finds; he was one of the first to realize the threats posed to many of the monuments from visitors, antiquarians, and nature.

Sites and work in the nineteenth century

The mid nineteenth century saw major advances in information gathering on the archaeological sites of Orkney, and not surprisingly the sites that were to become World Heritage Sites played a key role. Developments at this time benefited from a happy coincidence of several factors. Away from Orkney, antiquarian thought had been developing and various books published. In 1851

137

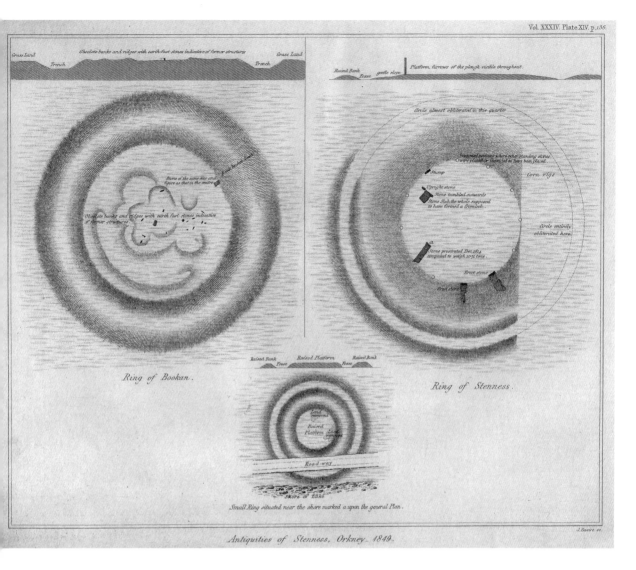

Ring of Bookan.

Ring of Stenness.

Antiquities of Stenness, Orkney. 1849.

Daniel Wilson published the *Archaeology and Prehistoric Annals of Scotland*, which was to become a key text. Wilson drew upon studies elsewhere in order to provide some chronological order for Scottish antiquities, notably Ellesmere's 1848 translation from the Danish of Thomsen's 'Three Age System'.[5] Works such as these allowed people to develop a better idea of the context of antiquities as well as a clearer archaeological chronology.

In Orkney, these advances in thought coincided with a sharp rise in the number of known archaeological sites due to the agricultural improvements and economic situation of the nineteenth century, which brought new land into cultivation. Orkney in the nineteenth century had a flourishing cultural and intellectual life: the grammar school and the library had long been founded (Kirkwall Grammar School is first mentioned in 1486, and the Library was founded in 1683). In 1854 the local paper, the Orcadian, was established.

FIGURE 75.
Detail of the Ring of Bookan and the Stones of Stenness from Thomas' survey.

COURTESY OF THE ORKNEY LIBRARY AND ARCHIVE PHOTOGRAPHIC LIBRARY

Not surprisingly, considerable interest was kindled in the local antiquities, and in the new ways to study and draw interpretations about them. Improvements in publication and the media facilitated the spread of information while progress in transport allowed those who wished to visit the islands to see the sites at first hand.

Local antiquarians

There were several key players who worked together in Orkney throughout the nineteenth century and thus fuelled a general interest in archaeology that has formed a lasting basis up to the present day. Standards varied in accordance with the norms of the time, but many sites were investigated and detailed accounts of local archaeology were produced. George Petrie, the local sheriff clerk and factor for the Graemeshall estate, lived locally, and he explored sites across Orkney. He conducted over 30 excavations and kept meticulous books and diaries which still form an important source of information today. James

FIGURE 76.
Skara Brae, shortly after it was discovered, as depicted by John Cairns for George Petrie's original publication of the site in the *Proceedings of the Society of Antiquaries of Scotland*, 1866.

COURTESY OF THE ORKNEY LIBRARY AND ARCHIVE PHOTOGRAPHIC LIBRARY

Proceedings of the Society of Antiquaries of Scotland

VOL. VII PLATE XXXIX.

Painted by John Cairns.

W. & A.K. Johnston Edinburgh.

Farrer was MP for Durham; he had a close friend in the Earl of Zetland, a major local landowner and he frequently visited Orkney. Petrie and Farrer worked together on several sites, including Maeshowe in 1861, and Farrer's illustrations provide a vivid account of the sites as they saw them. On occasion they were joined by Sir Henry Dryden, a famous architectural illustrator who recorded many of the sites.

Petrie's archaeology encompassed a broad interpretation of the past history of Orkney. He was one of the first to explore Skara Brae when it was revealed in 1850, and his work provides the first published account of the site (Figures 76, 77 and 78).[6] He recognized the importance of both Skara Brae and Maeshowe and he was able to set them into a wider context. He realized that the ancient monuments of Orkney represented a lengthy and varied timescale. Petrie, Farrer and Dryden were all enthusiastic Fellows of the Society of Antiquaries of Scotland in Edinburgh, and their work was published for the interest of antiquarians outside of Orkney as well as for local information. Orkney figured greatly in the nineteenth-century publications of the Society

FIGURE 77 (*below*). Petrie's original publication of Skara Brae included carefully measured plans and sections.

COURTESY OF THE ORKNEY LIBRARY AND ARCHIVE PHOTO-GRAPHIC LIBRARY

FIGURE 78 (*right*). Petrie's sections of Skara Brae.

COURTESY OF THE ORKNEY LIBRARY AND ARCHIVE PHOTO-GRAPHIC LIBRARY

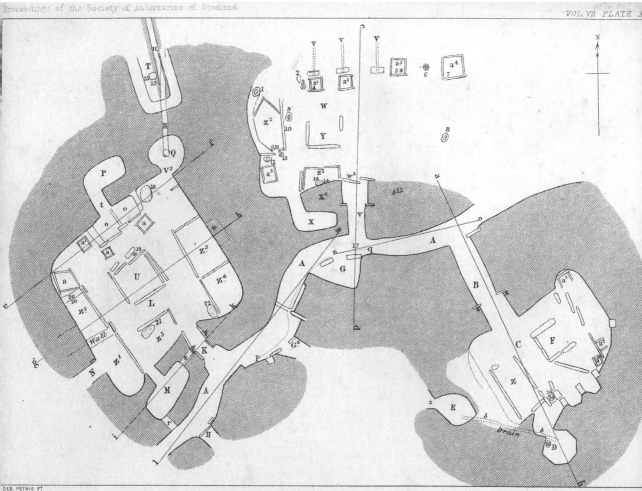

Proceedings of the Society of Antiquaries of Scotland.

VOL. VII. PLATE X

GEO. PETRIE F?

W.&A.K.Johnston Edin?

GROUND PLAN OF ANCIENT BUILDINGS AT SKARA, SKAILL, SANDWICK, ORKNEY.

Section on line a to b of Ground Plan.

Section on line c to d

Section on line e, f

Plan of Recess H.

Section on the line g, h.

Section on the line i, k,

View of line l, m northwest side of passage A. A.

View of line n, o, on N.W. side, being continuation of same passage

Section shewing west side of passage
or entrance with hole through flagstone
into cell M

View of line p, q, shewing entrances to Cell G, and passage Gn

GEO. PETRIE F.

W. & A.K. Johnston, Edinburgh

ELEVATIONS AND VIEWS OF ANCIENT BUILDINGS AT SKARA, SKAILL, SANDWICK, ORKNEY.
(ON THE LINES MARKED ON THE GROUND PLAN.)

of Antiquaries of Scotland and the work that was going on made an important contribution to the general understanding of the history of Scotland as
well as to the development of archaeological method and theory.

Popular interest in this work was stimulated by the increasing amount of
information on other societies around the world that came back from the
nineteenth-century explorers and scientists in areas such as the Americas
and Australia. Writers like Darwin fed the popular imagination with easily
accessible scientific accounts.[7] There was a general fascination with different,
'primitive', ways of life and archaeology provided a rich source of detail closer
to home that reminded nineteenth-century Britons not only of their own
romantic roots, but also of just how sophisticated they had become.

Towards the end of the nineteenth century excavation techniques and
recording began to develop further. The application of methods and theory
from other disciplines such as geology (from which the principals of stratigraphy were borrowed) considerably enhanced the budding profession of
archaeology. A greater understanding of chronology and context meant that it
was possible to recognize different time periods across a single site, and the
breadth of investigations was widened to include issues such as palaeobotany
and the world in which the people of the past had lived. There was a lot of
interest in the past and much excavation was undertaken by local landowners,
including William Traill in North Ronaldsay,[8] General Burroughs in Rousay,[9]
and R. S. Clouston in Stenness.[10]

The amount of archaeological information available was fast accumulating
and in 1922 the Orkney Antiquarian Society was founded. There was plenty
of local interest and educated voices to provide copy for lectures and publications. The Proceedings of the Orkney Society provided an important outlet for
information, but papers were also published further afield, such as in the
Proceedings of the Society of Antiquaries of Scotland.[11]

National government takes an interest

By the early twentieth century Orkney already had a well-established reputation not only for antiquities but also for those who studied them. It is not
surprising, therefore, that the two newly formed government bodies charged
with dealing with the antiquities of Britain took an interest in local sites. In
1906 the Ministry of Works took the Stones of Stenness into state care, and
sponsored some work there, mainly the re-erection of stones. It was at this
time that the infamous 'dolmen' was recreated. The Ring of Brodgar was taken
into care in the same year and Maeshowe soon followed, in 1910. Skara Brae
came into care in 1924 and consolidation work began here in 1927, under the
supervision of an archaeologist, Professor Gordon Childe, from Edinburgh
(Figures 79 and 80).

Closely following on the heels of Gordon Childe came the Royal
Commission on the Ancient and Historical Monuments of Scotland. They
were charged with making an inventory of all known archaeological sites in

FIGURE 79.
Skara Brae during the
excavations for the
Ministry of Works in
the 1920s.

THOMAS KENT,
COURTESY OF THE
ORKNEY LIBRARY AND
ARCHIVE
PHOTOGRAPHIC
LIBRARY

FIGURE 80.
Gordon Childe
excavating at Skara
Brae: Childe can be
seen emerging from the
hole on the left. This is
a very interesting
picture because it was
rare to catch Childe
smiling; the two ladies
to the right are clearly
joining in the work,
one holding a trowel –
though few female
volunteers today would
dig in a skirt.

THOMAS KENT,
COURTESY OF THE
ORKNEY LIBRARY AND
ARCHIVE
PHOTOGRAPHIC
LIBRARY

FIGURE 81.
Work at Skara Brae
involved the
construction of the first
sea wall. It still holds
good today, though
additions have been
made.

THOMAS KENT,
COURTESY OF THE
ORKNEY LIBRARY AND
ARCHIVE
PHOTOGRAPHIC
LIBRARY

Orkney. The task took them nine years and the inventory was finally published in 1946.[12] Although new sites have been discovered every year since publication of the RCAHMS inventory, it provided a timely reminder of the quality and quantity of archaeological sites in Orkney. RCAHMS also undertook some excavation, notably of sites in Eday and the Calf of Eday.

Debate over the age of Skara Brae

Although in the mid nineteenth century Wilson dated Skara Brae correctly to the Stone Age,[13] its age was to become the subject of considerable speculation in the early twentieth century. Childe's work revealed the complexity of the structural remains at Skara Brae, but he did not initially recognize just how old the site was, and when he published his excavations at the site in 1931 he entitled it *A Pictish Village in Orkney*. The age of Skara Brae became a matter for much debate between local antiquarians such as the historian Hugh Marwick[14] and English archaeologist Stuart Piggott[15] (who both got it right), and Edinburgh academics such as J. G. Callander, the Director of the National Museum of Antiquities, who supported Childe.[16] In the 1930s Childe went on to excavate a similar site at Rinyo in Rousay, accompanied by Walter Grant, a local landowner and whisky magnate,[17] and his findings here helped him to revise his opinions and recognize the antiquity of Skara Brae. Childe's contribution to archaeology was far-reaching:[18] his many publications formed the basis of much archaeological theory around the world,[19] and his work in Orkney formed an important part of this.[20]

Increased excavation in the early twentieth century

All of this archaeological activity had important spin-offs in terms of local employment and services. Walter Grant in Rousay began his archaeological work in the early 1930s and was responsible for the excavation of ten local chambered tombs and one broch. Initially Grant worked with J. G. Callander, from Edinburgh, but after Callander's death he worked alone using teams of local workmen, many of whom had considerable archaeological experience from other sites. Much of Grant's later work is still unpublished, but his notes help to fill out the picture of the past inhabitants of Orkney as well as providing a good idea of the state of preservation of some of the sites. Elsewhere, excavation included both local antiquarian projects such as that of Traill and Kirkness at the Knap of Howar in Papa Westray,[21] as well as projects led by the Ministry of Works at sites like the Brough of Birsay and the Broch of Gurness, which were being laid out for public presentation.

Although archaeological techniques had developed considerably since the mid nineteenth century they still fell far short of modern techniques. Many sites were unpublished and, even when they were written up, the analysis of material such as finds was often limited to the more 'interesting-looking' pieces. On the other hand, photographs, plans and section drawings were made and all helped to provide a lasting record of a site. Detailed site diaries often help to fill in the gaps where publication did not take place, and in some cases these provide interesting social history relating to the excavation teams. Orkney quickly developed a local labour force skilled in the ways of archaeology and tuned to the needs of the incoming archaeologists such as Childe. Many people today still remember stories from those who worked on sites such as Skara Brae in the 1920s and 30s.

Archaeology in the post-war years – from doldrums to development

Immediately after the Second World War, not surprisingly, archaeology saw a downturn in activity. In the 1950s Childe returned to excavate at the tombs of Maeshowe[22] and Quoyness,[23] and Orkney tombs formed an important part of Audrey Henshall's work on chambered tombs in Scotland, which was published in 1963.[24] Childe extended his work to look at the environment in the Neolithic, but investigations were in a state of semi-stagnation. However, everything was to change in the early 1970s with the development of radio-carbon dating, a method by which archaeologists could date their sites without having to resort to complex analysis of the stratigraphy, context and finds.[25] We know today that radiocarbon dating is not quite the panacea it at first seemed, but at the time the effect of the introduction of the new technique was revolutionary.[26] Old questions relating to the age of sites and development of society suddenly raised their heads once more and people needed to seek new sources of information or revisit old ones.

This process was enhanced by the development in these years of a battery of new techniques relating to archaeology. It was at this time that archaeology moved away from its roots as an art-historical discipline, in which pots or other artefacts were ordered through time so that we could trace the development of those who made them. Archaeology became a science with a suite of scientific techniques on which to draw. The profession fractured into many different specialisms. At the same time increased data fuelled new ways of thought. Archaeology also moved into the realm of social science as the theoreticians sought to understand the increasing evidence for the peoples of the past in terms of their behaviour, beliefs and sense of identity.[27]

The late twentieth century – a flourishing seed bed for research

In many ways these processes are still on-going. The seeds laid in the 1960s have taken root and grown. Orkney's archaeology still provides fertile ground for archaeologists to take advantage of new developments and even extend them. One of the first to arrive in the early 1970s was Professor Colin Renfrew (now Lord Renfrew of Kaimsthorn). Renfrew excavated at the tomb of Quanterness, at Maeshowe, and at the Ring of Brodgar.[28] His team included a suite of specialists who could apply the new techniques. At the same time David Clarke and Anna Ritchie arrived to excavate carefully placed trenches at Skara Brae,[29] and the Ritchies also worked at Knap of Howar[30] and the Stones of Stenness (Figure 82).[31] Teams from the University of Durham came to work at the Brough of Birsay[32] and in Deerness.[33] Orkney archaeology was thriving to the extent that a local excavation team, North of Scotland Archaeological Services (NOSAS), was based here under the leadership of John Hedges, who became well known for his work on burnt mounds such as Liddle and Beaquoy.[34] Work did not just include analysis of the sites; reconstruction of the past environment of Orkney was also important, both as a part of the archaeological studies and for stand-alone projects.[35]

Further projects were developed in the 1980s with Clarke's work at Noltland in Westray.[36] Westray saw the arrival of many large excavation teams: John Barber at Point of Cott;[37] Olwyn Owen at Tuquoy;[38] and Niall Sharples at Pierowall Quarry.[39] Other islands were not neglected, however; Bradford University was active in Sanday,[40] and several large projects took place in Mainland Orkney including on-going work by Colin Richards from Manchester University.[41] This influx of archaeologists had its own impact on island life. Some teams involved as many as 60 personnel, if only for short periods of time, which was a lot for an island with a population of perhaps

600, such as Westray. There was accommodation to be found, food to be provided, and the pub to stock. Several projects, such as that at Skara Brae, were high profile and resulted in television coverage. Orkney archaeology became highly visible, not only to the archaeologists and islanders but to people across Britain. This gave added impetus to local tourism which was, at the same time, developing rapidly.

The late twentieth and early twenty-first centuries have seen a dramatic rise in the popularity of archaeology, largely due to television programmes such as *Time Team.* The way that it has been presented means that people are interested not only in the results of archaeology, but also in the methods by which these results are achieved, and in the problems of managing and looking after the archaeological resource. Although there are sites and on-going excavations across Britain, Orkney now offers the opportunity to visit world-class sites and meet archaeologists in a particularly interesting and picturesque location. Organisations like the Friends of Orkney Archaeological Trust provide opportunities to volunteer on fieldwork as well as to attend expert lectures and fieldtrips, and these are well supported by both residents of the islands and by passing visitors. Many people find that voluntary participation flowers into a specialist interest and they become an essential part of local teams.

Archaeology enters the local infrastructure

In 1978 the Orkney Heritage Society appointed the first County Archaeologist, Dr Raymond Lamb. His appointment meant that a Sites and Monuments Record (SMR) could be created for Orkney, and this was an important step forward in managing the archaeological sites in the islands. Although archaeology is important to Orkney, the sites are but one of many, sometimes conflicting, interests that have to be taken into account in matters of development such as road improvements or house building. Lamb recorded many previously unknown sites and his SMR provided the first systematic update of the archaeological inventory made by RCAHMS in 1946.

Although the locally based archaeology unit, North of Scotland Archaeological Services, did not survive the 1980s, the last decades of the twentieth century saw archaeology in Orkney continue to flourish. Work took place on sites of all periods, and projects looked at such varying themes as burial, settlement and trade. This has generated a huge amount of data which can be utilised in the development of archaeological theory. Although some projects dating back as far as the 1970s have yet to be published, in general the wealth of the archaeological record in Orkney has been well exploited by those who research the past. This has resulted in the organization of two major international conferences in the islands: 'Neolithic Orkney in its European Context' in 1998;[42] and 'Sea Change, Iron Age Orkney' in 2001.[43] Unusually for academic conferences there were many local participants at both, as well as participants from across Europe, and both have since been published – no mean feat for a small island community.

FIGURE 82.
Excavations at the
Stones of Stenness in
the 1970s.

GRAHAM RITCHIE

FIGURE 83.
A team from Orkney
Archaeological Trust at
work.

ORKNEY
ARCHAEOLOGICAL
TRUST

FIGURE 84.
Geophysics taking place
in the World Heritage
Area.
ORKNEY
ARCHAEOLOGICAL
TRUST

FIGURE 85.
A television crew
filming at Mine Howe.
ORKNEY
ARCHAEOLOGICAL
TRUST

In 1996 archaeology in Orkney once more took a step forward with the setting-up of the Orkney Archaeological Trust (OAT), under the leadership of a new Island Archaeologist, Julie Gibson (Figure 83). OAT not only continues the SMR work, it works with the Council and other organizations on archaeological matters, carries out excavation work, and provides liaison and assistance for the many teams who still visit Orkney annually to carry out excavation, survey and other archaeological projects. In 1999 the archaeological presence in Orkney was consolidated with the formation of an Archaeology Department with Jane Downes at its head at the University of the Highlands and Islands Millennium Institute, housed in Orkney College in Kirkwall. It is now possible to train in Orkney as a professional archaeologist at postgraduate level.[44]

The early twenty-first century – new sites, new projects, new information

Unsurprisingly, archaeology is an active part of life in Orkney in the early twenty-first century. Despite the wealth of information that already exists, new sites are still uncovered every year and existing sites still provide new information. As this book was being written Miriam Cantley discovered a new Mesolithic site during fieldwork for her Masters degree. The site at Mine Howe was discovered in 1999 and a series of excavations led here by OAT uncovers new and surprising aspects of the site every year;[45] this site has blown apart most theories relating to Iron Age ritual practices. More new information about the Iron Age has come from Berstness in Westray, where excavations by Graeme Wilson and Hazel Moore are revealing a complex burial site.[46] In the World Heritage Area excavations by OAT at Ness of Brodgar have uncovered a range of Neolithic structures that was quite unexpected (Figure 84).[47]

In addition to those who journey to Orkney for work every year, a thriving community of local archaeologists has sprung up, and they are joined by an active group of local volunteers always ready to monitor a stretch of coastline, lend a hand in excavations, wash pot fragments, or sort bones.[48] The Council-run museum service has been rebranded as Orkney Museums and Heritage[49] and they work closely with those who excavate in order to conserve and analyse finds as well as providing important storage and display space. There are frequent lectures both from resident and visiting archaeologists and younger members of the community are catered for by a thriving Young Archaeologists' Club as well as by a considerable archaeological input to the school curriculum. Schoolchildren in Orkney visit many sites and their practical projectwork on topics such as the Stone Age or the Vikings is enhanced by specialists and museum professionals.

A measure of the interest in archaeology in Orkney lies in the regular contributions to local newspapers,[50] not only with excavation news but also with more in-depth examinations of archaeological issues. In addition, BBC Radio

Orkney broadcasts a popular archaeology magazine programme, Orky-ology, through the winter.[51]

The impact of archaeology in Orkney is felt further afield too. This is not only a professional matter, as information from Orkney continues to be used to develop and refine theory and interpretation; it is also to do with the continuing popularization of archaeology. Archaeology is well established as a popular subject for television, but it is important to keep the momentum going. Television requires a constant stream of new ideas. Orkney sites and projects are fashionable and visual, helped of course by the natural setting of the islands. Orkney archaeology is frequently to be seen as the backdrop on straightforward information programmes, and it is a common ingredient of more active excavation coverage (Figure 85).

Other coverage of archaeology can be more unexpected: in 2005 the Ring of Brodgar featured on a series of stamps issued by the Royal Mail. It is not surprising to find that archaeology has been promoted as a major attraction for those who visit Orkney for pleasure.

World Heritage status

The apogee of this attraction (to date) might therefore be seen as the designation of World Heritage Sites in Orkney. There is no doubt that a World Heritage designation carries a lot of status and is widely recognized.[52] Ironically, it is perhaps of more value to the non-archaeologist than to the archaeologist. For the non-archaeologist it provides a clear marker to something that has been deemed praiseworthy by those in the know. Archaeologists, on the other hand, continue to champion those sites that represent their own pet periods, or offer the potential to fill frustrating gaps in their knowledge. A World Heritage designation can be seen as just another layer of bureaucracy within which the professional has to work. The next (and final) chapter will look at the World Heritage designation in more detail.

World Heritage Status: The Ultimate Accolade?

....

Spiritual significance?

The Ring of Brodgar, the Stones of Stenness and Maeshowe were clearly very important to those who built them. They were special places, visited and revisited to reaffirm the connection between the communities of the day, their ancestors, the land and their future. Down the millennia these sites have continued to be special. They have been visited for pleasure and even, on occasions, used for ceremony, despite the fact that over the years the original links to the gods who presided over the sites have long gone. At midsummer 2005 the Ring of Brodgar was a busy place: an impromptu concert by John Kenny on the carnyx; a pagan wedding; and a cat lovers' celebration all took place in the space of 48 hours.

The sites generate their own sense of the sacred and this is often picked up by those who enter them, even today. Interestingly, research carried out by Angie McClanahan of Manchester University[1] found that for some Orcadians the experience of visiting the stones is something that affirms their links to the land. She also noted that visitors to Orkney often appreciate the wild, unspoilt nature of the sites, especially the Ring of Brodgar, and that many find that this awakens feelings of spirituality.

The sites are still important today. Britain in the early twenty-first century is a society where heritage has come to be, for some, a new religion. It acts as a motivating force that provides both meaning and purpose to life, for varied reasons. Perhaps foremost among these is the strong relationship which exists between spirituality and belonging. Many people visit heritage sites to learn about their ancestors and affirm their place as a Briton. The great time depth that is available and Britain's long history of invasion and settlement means that this feeling of belonging applies to all who wish to find it. No matter where your ancestors came from and when,[2] it is possible at some point to identify with the period at which your family may have entered Britain. People can look back to understand the roots of the society their predecessors knew, and into which they integrated. More prosaic, perhaps, is the financial side of heritage. It has been said that we have become a commercial species, always eager to make money out of something. Heritage, with its experiences and

World Heritage Status: The Ultimate Accolade?

souvenir stalls, has become an important part of this, ever ready to relieve us of cash. It is not only to be found among the ancient sites we visit. The use of 'heritage' to add value to products from cheese to new homes is now widespread. There have been connections between religion and commerce since biblical times, and no doubt before, but it is a strange irony to see it come full circle at sites as early as Stonehenge.[3]

The experience of those who visit the sites in Orkney, and elsewhere, today is in many ways no less religious or spiritual than that of those who entered these monuments in the past, even if the focus of their visits has changed. The designation of the remains as of World Heritage status is a clear affirmation of their importance in the twenty-first century. This is an importance that has endured for some 5,000 years. We carefully ascribe the building and status of the monuments to a stratified society in the Neolithic (Chapter Six), but it is equally important to examine who decides today whether somewhere is worthy of World Heritage status, and on what

FIGURE 86.
Skara Brae has clearly been a tourist attraction for some time, as this photograph from 1955 shows.

COURTESY OF UNIVERSITY OF DUNDEE ARCHIVE SERVICES

grounds. We need to know what it means, and to consider whether World Heritage status has changed things in Orkney.

What is World Heritage?

In 1972 a World Heritage Convention was adopted by the grand conference of UNESCO and it has been signed to date by 175 countries.[4] The United Kingdom signed in 1984. The World Heritage Convention seeks to safeguard the well-being of exceptional sites of cultural and natural value. In the eyes of those who drew up the convention these sites provide a 'common global heritage' and should be 'treasured as unique testimonies to an enduring past'.[5] The convention recognises that the long-term future of many of these sites is threatened and sees their preservation as something that should concern us all.[6] UNESCO encourages countries to sign the Convention and look after their own heritage, and also encourages them to put forward outstanding sites for inclusion in the World Heritage List. Whether or not a site is included on the list is decided by a committee of 21 members, the World Heritage Committee. World Heritage is divided into cultural and natural aspects, and the sites in Orkney fall under the heading of cultural heritage, defined as 'a monument, group of buildings or site of historical, aesthetic, archaeological, scientific, ethnological or anthropological value'.[7]

Nomination for the World Heritage List

The 21 members of the World Heritage Committee are elected for six years with seven members changing every two years. The Committee meets once a year to decide on new sites as well as on various matters relating to existing sites and procedure.

The process regarding new World Heritage Sites is lengthy and bureaucratic, taking about 18 months to complete. Individual countries first need a general overview of all cultural and natural properties that might be of outstanding universal value. From this they select properties for nomination. A nomination document must then be drawn up to identify the site or sites, explain why they have been put forward, describe them, outline management issues (including interpretation), and look at factors such as future monitoring of the sites. The nomination document for the Heart of Neolithic Orkney comprises 62 pages and is lavishly illustrated.[8]

After nomination the documents are checked by the World Heritage Centre to see whether they are complete and then they are forwarded for evaluation. The International Council for Monuments and Sites (ICOMOS) is responsible for the evaluation of cultural sites. They send a team of experts to visit the site and prepare a report on aspects such as the importance of the site as well as its management. They have to assess whether it is of outstanding universal value.

The evaluation then goes for examination before an executive body, the

World Heritage Bureau, which is composed of seven members of the World Heritage Committee.[9] This is the body that will decide whether or not to recommend the property for nomination; sometimes they may ask for more information. The World Heritage Bureau then pass information back to the World Heritage Committee, who make the final decision as to whether a site should be inscribed on the World Heritage List.

The International Council for Monuments and Sites (ICOMOS)

Although inscription is actually carried out by a UNESCO committee, the body most associated with World Heritage sites is ICOMOS, 'an international, non-governmental organization dedicated to the conservation of the world's historic monuments and sites. The organization was founded in 1965, as a result of the international adoption of the Charter for the Conservation and Restoration of Monuments and Sites in Venice in the previous year. Today the organization has National Committees in over 107 countries'.[10]

ICOMOS acts as the main advisor for UNESCO on all matters regarding cultural heritage. It manages 21 international committees which seek to establish international standards for the management of cultural heritage worldwide. In many ways ICOMOS acts as a forum which promotes professional dialogue, the exchange of information and education; it helps with training programmes and represents a body of highly qualified professionals. One of the main strands of its work is to advise UNESCO on new properties for the World Heritage List and on the existing management of those properties already on the List. ICOMOS also seeks to encourage public interest and awareness of cultural heritage.

It is possible to join ICOMOS as a member. There are both institutional and individual members and the list of potential individual membership is long: 'Individual members shall be open to any individual engaged in the conservation of monuments, groups of buildings and sites as a member of the scientific, technical or administrative staff of national, regional or local monuments, fine arts or antiquities services, a decision-maker or a specialist engaged in the conservation, restoration, rehabilitation and enhancement of monuments, groups of buildings and sites, including, as appropriate, architects, town planners, historians, archaeologists, ethnologists, and archivists'.[11]

Why the Heart of Neolithic Orkney?

The Orkney monuments were only the third World Heritage Site to be inscribed for Scotland. In 1986 St Kilda was inscribed as a natural site and in 2005 it was inscribed on cultural grounds as well, making it one of very few sites worldwide to hold both cultural and natural values.[12] Edinburgh Old and New Towns were inscribed in 1996,[13] Orkney was inscribed in 1999, and New Lanark was added in 2001.[14] The Heart of Neolithic Orkney is, to date, the only site inscribed purely for its archaeological value.

FIGURE 87.
Life goes on at the
Stones of Stenness.
C. WICKHAM-JONES

The statement of significance provided by Historic Scotland, which nominated the monuments, proclaims them a 'triumph of the human spirit in early ages and in isolated places'[15] (though I wonder whether Orkney was isolated in the Neolithic). It looks both at the achievement of building them and at their good state of preservation. Maeshowe is seen as 'an expression of genius within a group of people whose other tombs were claustrophobic chambers in smaller mounds'[16] (some of us might seek to discuss this view, however). The Stones of Stenness 'is a unique and early expression of the major ritual customs of the people who buried their dead in tombs like Maeshowe'.[17] The Ring of Brodgar 'is the finest known truly circular late Neolithic or early Bronze Age stone ring'[18] (I'm glad they got it right when laying it out!). Skara Brae, meanwhile, is noted for its remarkable preservation, for the stone-built furniture, and for its artefacts, all of which provide a rich source of information.[19]

FIGURE 88.
Aerial view of the Ring
of Brodgar.

JOHN LEITH

Historic Scotland goes on to justify the inscription of the monuments. Both the creative genius of their builders and their access to a rich tradition of similar monuments across Britain are cited. The statement talks of the significance of the indigenous cultural tradition which the monuments represent. Interestingly, though a decision was taken not to put forward the landscape between the monuments for inscription with World Heritage status, Historic Scotland does mention it here as being of outstanding value.[20]

As we can see, the statements by Historic Scotland are not without controversy, but they do provide forceful reasoning as to the position of the monuments of the Heart of Neolithic Orkney among other heritage sites in Scotland. Quite simply, Skara Brae, the Ring of Brodgar, the Stones of Stenness and Maeshowe are exceptional places, both in the context of the times in which they were first used and in the context of today.

After inscription: what then?

The Heart of Neolithic Orkney was inscribed on the World Heritage List in 1999. What happened next? Has it made any difference to the sites? English

Heritage says that World Heritage status brings prestige and more visitors.[21] It should ensure the highest qualities of interpretation, and improved protection.

One of the first duties of a state after inscription is to draw up a management plan to ensure the future well-being of the site, and this was done for Neolithic Orkney in 2001.[22] All of the Orkney sites are owned and managed by the state, through Historic Scotland, but management is not a simple matter. The sites mean little in isolation, and it is important to look after the landscape around them. Two buffer zones have thus been drawn up around the sites, an Inner Buffer Zone and an Outer Buffer Zone. These are based on pre-existing designations and each has its own management ideals.[23] The buffer zones are geographically wide-ranging, and many different organisations and individuals are involved, from local farmers and householders to businesses and Orkney Islands Council. The bureaucracy involved with World Heritage Sites does not stop with nomination.

In Britain World Heritage status does not carry any enhanced statutory controls. The management in Orkney's case involves a steering group set up to implement the management plan. Any short-term specific issues are addressed by project groups, brought into being when needed. There is also a consultation group which seeks to involve local interest groups and residents. The steering group for Orkney includes both cultural and natural advisors and the management plan is all-embracing. It includes elements such as tourism and rural conservation, as well as specific work to the sites. Regular updates on current work are provided by Historic Scotland on their website, where it is possible to register for information on the consultation group and obtain copies of the Management Plan.[24]

The impact of World Heritage status for visitors and site managers is already being felt, with steps such as upgrading of car-parking facilities for Maeshowe and the appointment of rangers to help tourists. It will be a long process and World Heritage status does not, of itself, bring additional funding, but it is clear that it has provided a forceful accolade of which the powers that be will take notice.

The missing landscape

At this point it is worth considering omissions from the World Heritage Nomination in Orkney. The sites put forward for nomination are all monuments which are owned and managed by Historic Scotland, known as Properties in Care. As a result, official maps of the Orkney World Heritage Sites comprise isolated dots on the landscape.[25] Yet these sites did not exist in isolation. The people of the Neolithic inhabited a world; they were influenced by their environment and in turn helped to shape it. Although archaeology used to concentrate on the sites themselves, researchers now take the wider world into account and related subjects such as the environmental sciences and aspects of perception are important.[26]

The omission of the wider cultural landscape of Orkney has been noted by academics.[27] It also makes life very difficult for those who work at a more popular level. It is hard to explain the significance of those tracts of land between the sites to visitors when they are not, apparently, regarded as of equal significance with the sites themselves. This is curious given the proliferation of traces recorded by recent geophysics in the area.[28] It is also hard to explain why the reconstructed remains of Barnhouse were not regarded as of equal value with the reconstructed henge at the Stones of Stenness in the adjacent field.

There are, of course, good management reasons for creating a World Heritage Site that comprised only Historic Scotland's own properties. Yet the creation of buffer zones suggests that it is not as simple as that. It is as important to control development between and around the sites as on them.[29]

The local community

The impact of World Heritage status for the Orkney community is, in some ways, elusive. Despite the existence of websites such as http://www.worldheritagesite.org/, research has yet to show whether inscription has drawn significantly more visitors to Orkney. The sites and monuments of Orkney have been well known for at least 200 years, judging by the writing of people like Barry.[30] He was writing for those who would not be able to travel easily, but improved transport has since made tourism an integral part of island culture, though the current costs of air flights do little to help that. In our time-conscious age many visitors are not keen to sacrifice the time necessary to travel north by train, bus, or car and take the boat. Nevertheless, tourism does provide much-needed income for the islands' economy.

For those who live within or near to the buffer zones the impact on their lives is still more direct. They must now take account of the management needs of the sites as they go about their daily lives. For some this is not a problem, others find it more difficult. All are invited to participate in regular consultation group meetings, which can sometimes get quite heated.

In many ways the impact of designation has been disappointing for those who live around the World Heritage sites. There seems to have been a general perception that designation would bring increased funding to deal with problems like overcrowded car-parking, the need to improve interpretation, and better visitor facilities. Some thought that appreciably more visitors would quickly be attracted to the sites, thus improving the possibilities of making a living from the 'heritage industry'. In the first few years since designation it sometimes seems as if the main impact has been negative: an increase of bureaucracy, rather than a positive effect on lifestyles and perceptions.

The difference for the archaeological community

The impact on local life may have been questionable, but what of the impact on those heritage professionals who live and work in Orkney? For Historic Scotland the effects of World Heritage have been tangible. In addition to the work involved in nomination, they have now the additional work involved in producing a management plan, implementing and updating it, and working with local bodies and individuals across the area. Physical projects like traffic management have to be attended to. It could be argued, however, that given the importance of the sites this sort of work should have been taking place anyway, so that designation has merely created the atmosphere in which to facilitate it.

Historic Scotland is but one of the bodies that works in the heritage field in Orkney. Two other important organisations are the Orkney Archaeological Trust (OAT) and Orkney Museums and Heritage. Designation has inevitably brought more work for them as it has added to the international importance and the research potential of the sites. Both OAT and Orkney Museums and Heritage also liaise with Historic Scotland regarding the management of the sites. Increased awareness has also provided more work, in the shape of advice to the many television crews and others who seek to use Orkney sites for documentary and other purposes.

Further afield, a wider world of people has been affected, namely the research community of archaeologists who seek to understand better the worlds of the past. It is always possible that designation might stifle work elsewhere by focusing research into the narrow band of World Heritage sites at the expense of others. This does not appear to have happened; one could argue that designation has actually improved the situation in Orkney. The research potential of the existing remains at Skara Brae and other sites has long been apparent. This has led to a negative impact on some studies in the past, such as those of Mesolithic or Bronze Age Orkney, but designation has brought about the need for a broader understanding of the context of the sites and their role through the ages. In this way, less well-studied periods such as these have been given a boost because it is possible to identify them as important gaps in the understanding of Orkney through the ages. Work on the Research Agenda for the World Heritage sites has allowed archaeologists to stand back and take a broad view of the prehistory and history of the islands.

For many the question is: can we interpret the archaeology of Orkney through a narrow group of sites? The answer has to be yes, as long as we look at them in the broadest sense. World Heritage designation has given added impetus to the archaeology, and while it has not of itself brought increased funding, work on elements like the Research Agenda has both highlighted the many possibilities for further archaeological work, and provided a useful tool for those who assess funding applications. Designation has given both focus and impetus to the study and management of the archaeology of Orkney.

Added protection

In addition to the direct effects within Orkney of another layer of bureaucratic designation to be considered, there are wider, less direct, effects. One of these has been the inclusion of the Heart of Neolithic Orkney on the list of British Sites worthy of protection in time of war. The list was originally drawn up in 1954, and is known as the Hague Convention.[31] It has been ratified by some 114 countries around the world and is designed to avoid the destruction of cultural sites. In 2005 Britain has finally moved towards ratification of the Convention and made the first steps towards drawing up its own list of cultural sites.

World Heritage Sites in Britain

The Heart of Neolithic Orkney is but one of 25 World Heritage sites in Britain and Ireland. The majority of these are cultural. Interestingly, three sites relate to Neolithic ritual complexes: the Heart of Neolithic Orkney; Stonehenge and Avebury; and Newgrange and the Bend of the Boyne. No other archaeological period or culture has been recognised in this way. We may be some 5,000 years removed from our Neolithic ancestors, but their impact on modern life is unquestionable.

It is all very well to designate sites; the value of designation lies in their well-being. As the fire of 2003 in the Old Town of Edinburgh (another World Heritage Site) shows, management is not always easy. It is no small matter for a country to nominate a site, and many countries take it as a great honour to have World Heritage Sites.

FIGURE 89.
Sunset atop the
Brodgar stones.
SIGURD TOWRIE

The end?

In the end the main judges of World Heritage Status can only be ourselves, the visitors. We are all visitors in relation to these sites, whether we use them for a living or for relaxation. Do we plod wearily from site to site, or forge ahead eager to immerse ourselves in the fading world of 5,000 years ago? Do we gain from the 'visitor experience', or concentrate on a cup of coffee to fortify ourselves for the next dose of culture? Will we look after the sites for the future, even nominate more World Heritage Sites? Heritage is important in Orkney and to our lives everywhere. Can we make use of it to understand these islands and, perhaps, ourselves, a little more?

CHAPTER THIRTEEN

Moving On

....

Visiting the sites

The monuments of the Heart of Neolithic Orkney are all well signed from the main road that runs between Kirkwall and Stromness. Each has a car park and there is a café and heritage centre at Skara Brae. In addition, several tour companies offer trips to the sites, mostly setting off from Kirkwall. It is also possible to visit the sites using public transport.

The Ring of Brodgar and the Stones of Stenness are free and open for visits at any time of day (or night). Charges are made at Skara Brae and Maeshowe, at both of which visiting times are set by Historic Scotland. Further information can be obtained from Historic Scotland or Visit Orkney, the websites of both of which are listed below. Because of the limited size of the chamber at Maeshowe visitors are required to pre-book a guided tour from Historic Scotland. At Skara Brae you are free to wander for as long as you like. Skara Brae is twinned with the historic Skaill House, which lies a few hundred metres from the site, and the entry ticket allows admission to both locations.

The guide books listed below provide useful information for those wishing to visit other archaeological sites in Orkney.

Museums

Skara Brae has a good interpretation centre.
The Orkney Museum in Kirkwall is run by Orkney Museums and Heritage, the heritage branch of Orkney Islands Council, and it provides excellent displays relating to the ancient and not-so-ancient past of Orkney.
Stromness Museum is based on the collections of the Stromness Natural History Society and offers an eclectic mix from explorers to navigation, archaeology and natural history in a wonderful setting that provides a welcome respite from the tenets of modern museum design. There is a small charge for visiting Stromness Museum.
The *National Museum of Scotland* on Chambers Street in Edinburgh has an archaeology section which puts Neolithic Orkney into a wider setting.

Further Reading

The World Heritage Sites that form the Heart of Neolithic Orkney appear in many publications, from novels to guidebooks, and include many academic discussions. The following selection will lead you to other publications. Also included are some general guidebooks to set the scene for Orkney and its flora and fauna. Specific references to material in the text are listed in Notes to the Chapters.

Novels and stories

Fidler, K. (2005) *The Boy with the Bronze Axe*, Kelpie, Floris Books, Edinburgh. A good read for 8–12 year olds.

Mitchison, N. (1987) *Early in Orcadia*, R. Drew, London. A novel for adults.

Muir, T. (1998) *The Mermaid Bride and other Orkney Folk Tales*, The Orcadian, Kirkwall. A collection of traditional folk tales.

Scott, Sir W. (1822) *The Pirate*, Constable, Edinburgh. Scott's classic story of piracy is set in Orkney and Shetland and includes descriptions of the Stones of Stenness and the Odin Stone.

Woodbridge, T. (1988) *Sheldra, a Child in Neolithic Orkney*, Tempus Reparatum, Oxford. Life in Skara Brae described for younger children.

In addition the Orkney poet George Mackay Brown wrote numerous stories set among the antiquities of Orkney and all are a good read. A complete list of his works may be found on http://www.georgemackaybrown.co.uk/.

General academic publications and popular guidebooks

Historic Scotland have published a series of guidebooks related to their properties in care. With relation to the Heart of Neolithic Orkney, existing texts on *Skara Brae* and on *Maeshowe* are likely to be upgraded with other texts relating to the World Heritage Sites and their setting.

Ashmore, P. J. (1996) *Neolithic and Bronze Age Scotland*, Historic Scotland and BT Batsford, London.

Barry, G. (1805) *History of the Orkney Islands*, Constable, Edinburgh (reprinted 1975 by the Mercat Press, Edinburgh).

Berry, R. J. (1985) *The Natural history of Orkney*, Collins, London (The New Naturalist Library).

Berry, R. J. and Firth, H. N. eds (1986) *The People of Orkney*, The Orkney Press, Kirkwall (Aspects of Orkney, 4).

Booth, C., Cuthbert, M. and Reynolds, P. (1984) *The Birds of Orkney*, The Orkney Press, Kirkwall.

Bullard, E. (1995) *Wildflowers in Orkney, a new checklist*, privately published, Kirkwall.

Burgher, L. (1991) *Orkney, an illustrated architectural guide*, Royal Incorporation of Architects in Scotland, Edinburgh.

Childe, V. G. (1931) *Skara Brae, a Pictish Village in Orkney*, Kegan Paul, London.

Davidson, J. L. and Henshall, A. S. (1989) *The Chambered Tombs of Orkney*, Edinburgh University Press, Edinburgh.

Downes, J., Foster, S. and Wickham-Jones, C. R., with Jude Callister eds (2005) *The Heart of Neolithic Orkney World Heritage Site, Research Agenda*, Historic Scotland, Edinburgh (this document may be freely downloaded from the Historic Scotland website).

Downes, J. and Ritchie, A. eds (2003) *Sea Change, Orkney and Northern Europe in the Late Iron Age AD 300–800*, Pinkfoot Press, Angus.

Fenton, A. (1978) *The Northern Isles: Orkney and Shetland*, John Donald, Edinburgh.

Garnham, T. (2004) *Lines on the Landscape, Circles from the Sky*, Tempus, Gloucester.

Hedges, J. W. (1984) *Tomb of the Eagles, a Window on Stone Age Tribal Britain*, John Murray Ltd, London.

Historic Scotland (1998) *Nomination of the Heart of Neolithic Orkney for Inclusion in the World Heritage List*, Historic Scotland, Edinburgh.

Hjaltalin, H. J. and Goudie, G. trans (1977) *The Orkneyinga Saga*, The Mercat Press, Edinburgh (facsimile of the 1873 edition published by Edmonston and Douglas).

Low, G. (1774) *Orkney and Schetland 1774*, Melven Press, Inverness (a recent reprint).

Renfrew, A. C. ed. (1985) *The Prehistory of Orkney*, Edinburgh University Press, Edinburgh.

Ritchie, A. (1985) *Exploring Scotland's Heritage, Orkney and Shetland*, The Stationery Office, Edinburgh.

Ritchie, A. (1995) *Prehistoric Orkney*, Historic Scotland and BT Batsford, London.

Ritchie, A. (1996) *Orkney*, The Stationery Office, Edinburgh.

Ritchie, A. ed. (2000) *Neolithic Orkney in its European Context*, McDonald Institute Monographs, Cambridge.

Ritchie, A. and Ritchie, G. (1995) *The Ancient Monuments of Orkney*, The Stationery Office, Edinburgh.

Wickham-Jones, C. R. (1998) *Orkney a Historical Guide*, Birlinn, Edinburgh.

Websites

Papers and pictures in honour of Daphne Hume Lorimer.

http://www.orkneydigs.org.uk/DHL/papers/cwj/index.html

The website of Orkney Archaeological Trust is not very informative, but this selection of papers is a treasure trove of personal and academic information inspired by one of Orkney's best loved archaeologists.

Orkneyjar, the heritage of the Orkney islands

http://www.orkneyjar.com/

Orkneyjar is run by local journalist Sigurd Towrie, whose knowledge of Orkney and its past is encyclopaedic.

Charles Tait

http://www.charles-tait.co.uk/

Excellent images of Orkney together with general information.

Maeshowe

http://www.maeshowe.co.uk/

Charles Tait sets up his webcam inside Maeshowe every year so that people around the world can view the setting sun as it strikes into the heart of the chamber.

Visit Orkney

http://www.visitorkney.com/

Visit Orkney's website provides useful tourist information for those wanting to visit the islands.

Orkney Museums and Heritage

http://www.orkney.gov.uk/nqcontent.cfm?a_id=443

The website of the Orkney Islands Council Museums and Heritage Services with images, information, maps and a whole lot more.

Orkney Communities Website

http://www.orkneycommunities.co.uk/index.asp

The place to find out about events in Orkney and organisations such as the Friends of Orkney Archaeological Trust who provide local lectures and other events as well as a regular newsletter.

Historic Scotland

http://www.historic-scotland.gov.uk/

A wide range of information, from World Heritage sites in Scotland to visiting archaeological sites and information on radiocarbon dates.

The Royal Commission on the Ancient and Historic Monuments of Scotland

http://www.rcahms.gov.uk/search.html

Once you have taken that holiday in Orkney this site will help you to look for more information about all the archaeological humps and bumps that you passed.

Council for Scottish Archaeology

http://www.britarch.ac.uk/csa/

This website is for those who wish to find out more about Scottish Archaeology, including how to participate in archaeological events or join a local society.

The Council for British Archaeology

http://www.britarch.ac.uk/

The gateway to information about archaeology in Britain including subscriptions to the popular magazine *British Archaeology*.

ICOMOS

http://www.icomos.org/

The website for the International Council on Monuments and Sites is full of information relating to World Heritage sites around the globe.

Notes to the Chapters

Chapter One: Orkney and its World Heritage

1. W. Mykura (1976) *British Regional Geology: Orkney and Shetland*, HMSO, Edinburgh.
2. J. Bunting (1994) 'Vegetation history of Orkney, Scotland: pollen records from two small basins in west Mainland', *New Phytologist* **128**, 771–92.
3. V. G. Childe (1931) *Skara Brae, a Pictish Village in Orkney*, Kegan Paul, London.
4. D. V. Clarke (2004) 'The construction of narratives for Neolithic Scotland', in *Scotland in Ancient Europe*, eds I. Shepherd and G. Barclay, Society of Antiquaries of Scotland, Edinburgh, 46–7.
5. E. MacKie (1977) *Science and Society in Prehistoric Britain*, Paul Elek, London; E. MacKie (1997) 'Maeshowe and the winter solstice: ceremonial aspects of the Orkney Grooved Ware culture', *Antiquity* **71**, 338–59.
6. C. Richards (2005) 'The Great Stone Circles Project', *British Archaeology* **81**, 16–21.
7. S. Towrie (n.d.) 'Building the Stone Circles', *Orkneyjar* (http://www.orkneyjar.com/history/brodgar/building.htm) (visited August 2005).
8. E. MacKie (2005) 'Maeshowe and the winter solstice: ceremonial aspects of the Orkney Grooved Ware culture', *Antiquity* **71**, 338–59.
9. A. Challands, T. Muir and C. Richards (2005) 'The Great Passage Grave of Maeshowe, The Standing Stone', in *Dwelling Among the Monuments*, ed. C. Richards, MacDonald Institute Monographs, Cambridge, 242–4.
10. A. Challands, T. Muir and C. Richards (2005) 'The Great Passage Grave of Maeshowe, Maeshowe Platform', in *Dwelling Among the Monuments*, ed. C. Richards, MacDonald Institute Monographs, Cambridge, 235–42.
11. J. Farrer (1862) *Notice of Runic Inscriptions Discovered During Recent Excavations in the Orkneys*, Edinburgh.
12. M. P. Barnes (1994) *The Runic Inscriptions of Orkney*, Uppsala University, Uppsala.
13. B. Ballin Smith and G. Petersen (2004) 'Brodgar, Stenness', *Discovery and Excavation in Scotland 2003*, 102–3.
14. N. Card and S. Ovenden (2005) 'World Heritage Area', *Discovery and Excavation in Scotland 2004*, 97.
15. N. Card (2005) 'Neolithic Orkney', in *The Heart of Neolithic Orkney World Heritage Site Research Agenda*, eds J. Downes, S. Foster, C. R. Wickham-Jones and J. Callister, Historic Scotland, Edinburgh, 55–6.

Chapter Two: The People Before: Mesolithic Orkney

1. C. R. Wickham-Jones, A. Clarke and A. Barlow (1986) 'A Project in Experimental Archaeology, Avasjo 1982', *Rosc* **2**, 97–104.
2. R. Bradley (2000) *The Archaeology of Natural Places*, Routledge, London.
3. Council for Scottish Archaeology (2001) *The Archaeological Resource and the Historic Environment – balancing conservation with development*, Edinburgh.
4. N. Card (2005) 'History of Prehistoric Research', in *The Heart of Neolithic Orkney World Heritage Site Research Agenda*, eds J. Downes, S. Foster, C. R. Wickham-Jones and J. Callister, Historic Scotland, Edinburgh, 40–6.
5. N. Card, J. Downes and S. Ovenden (2005) 'Mine Howe Environs', *Discovery and Excavation in Scotland 2004*, 96–7.
6. C. R. Wickham-Jones (2004) 'The Mesolithic in Scotland: action archaeology for the twenty-first century', *Before Farming* **2004/1**, article 3 (http://www.waspress.co.uk/journals).
7. J. Bunting (1994) 'Vegetation history of Orkney, Scotland: pollen records from two small basins in west Mainland', *New Phytologist* **128**, 771–92.
8. S. Towrie (2003) 'Experts ponder mystery of Neolithic wooden structure', *Orkneyjar* (http://www.orkneyjar.com/archaeology/wideford.htm) (visited August 2005).

9. C. Dickson (2000) 'The decline of woodland in Orkney: early Neolithic to late Iron Age', in *People as Agents of Environmental Change*, eds R. Nicholson and T. O'Connor, Oxbow Books, Oxford, 37–44.

10. S. Dawson and D. E. Smith (1997) 'Holocene Relative Sea Level Changes on the margin of a glacio-isostatically uplifted area: an example from northern Caithness, Scotland', *The Holocene* 7, 1, 59–77.

11. D. E. Smith, A. C. De La Vega and S. Dawson (1996) 'Relative sea level changes in Orkney' in *The Quaternary of Orkney: Field Guide*, ed. A. M. Hall, Quaternary Research Association, Cambridge, 16–19.

12. C. Ballantyne (2004) 'After the ice: paraglacial and postglacial evolution of the physical environment of Scotland 20,000 to 5,000 BP', in *Mesolithic Scotland and its Neighbours*, ed. A. Saville, Society of Antiquaries of Scotland, Edinburgh, 27–44.

13. K. J. Edwards (2004) 'Palaeoenvironments of the Late Upper Palaeolithic and Mesolithic periods in Scotland and the North Sea area: new work, new thoughts', in *Mesolithic Scotland and its Neighbours*, ed. A. Saville, Society of Antiquaries of Scotland, Edinburgh, 55–72.

14. A. G. Dawson and D. E. Smith (1990) 'Evidence for a tsunami from a Mesolithic site in Inverness, Scotland', *Journal of Archaeological Science* 17, 6, 509–12.

15. S. Bondevik, J. Mangerud, S. Dawson, A. G. Dawson and O. Lohne (2003) 'Record-breaking height for 8000 yr old tsunami in the North Atlantic', *EOS (American Geophysical Union)* 84, 31, August 2003, 289–300.

16. N. Sharples (2000) 'Antlers and Orcadian rituals: an ambiguous role for red deer in the Neolithic', in *Neolithic Orkney in its European Context*, ed. A. Ritchie, MacDonald Institute Monographs, Cambridge, 107–17.

17. J. Hedges (1984) *Tomb of the Eagles*, John Murray, London.

Chapter Three: The Arrival of Change: The Early Neolithic

1. A. De La Vega-Leinert, D. H. Keen, R. L. Jones, J. M. Wells and D. E. Smith (2000) 'Mid-Holocene environmental changes in the Bay of Skaill, Mainland Orkney, Scotland: an integrated geomorphological, sedimentological and stratigraphical study', *Journal of Quaternary Science* 15, 509–28.

2. S. Jones and C. Richards (2000) 'Neolithic Cultures in Orkney: Classification and Interpretation', in *Neolithic Orkney in its European Context*, ed. A. Ritchie, McDonald Institute Monographs, Cambridge, 101–6.

3. N. Card (2005) 'Neolithic Orkney', in *The Heart of Neolithic Orkney World Heritage Site Research Agenda*, eds J. Downes, S. Foster, C. R. Wickham-Jones and J. Callister, Historic Scotland, Edinburgh, 55–6.

4. A. Jones (2000) 'Life after Death: Monuments, Material Culture and Social Change in Neolithic Orkney', in *Neolithic Orkney in its European Context*, ed. A. Ritchie, McDonald Institute Monographs, Cambridge, 127–38.

5. P. J. Ashmore (2005) 'Absolute Chronology', in *Scotland in Ancient Europe*, eds I. Shepherd and G. Barclay, Society of Antiquaries of Scotland, Edinburgh, 125–36.

6. A. Ritchie (1983) 'Excavation of a Neolithic farmstead at Knap of Howar, Papa Westray, Orkney', *Proceedings of the Society of Antiquaries of Scotland* 113, 40–121.

7. J. R. Hunter (2000) 'Pool, Sanday, and a Sequence for the Orcadian Neolithic', in *Neolithic Orkney in its European Context*, ed. A. Ritchie, McDonald Institute Monographs, Cambridge, 117–26.

8. J. L. Davidson and A. S. Henshall (1989) *The Chambered Cairns of Orkney*, Edinburgh University Press, Edinburgh.

9. J. Barber (2000) 'Death in Orkney: a Rare Event', in *Neolithic Orkney in its European Context*, ed. A. Ritchie, McDonald Institute Monographs, Cambridge, 185–7.

10. J. Hedges (1984) *Tomb of the Eagles*, John Murray, London.

11. C. Richards ed. (2005) *Dwelling Among the Monuments*, McDonald Institute Monographs, Cambridge.

Chapter Four: Skara Brae: Settling Down and Taming the Land in the Late Neolithic

1. F. Sturt (2005) 'Fishing for meaning: lived space and the early Neolithic of Orkney', in *Set in Stone*, eds V. Cummings and A. Pannett, Oxbow Books, Oxford, 68–80.

2. N. Sharples (2000) 'Antlers and Orcadian rituals: an ambiguous role for red deer in the Neolithic', in *Neolithic Orkney in its European Context*, ed. A. Ritchie, McDonald Institute Monographs, Cambridge, 107–17.

3. M. Richards (2005) 'The Early Neolithic in Britain: new insights from biomolecular archaeology', in *Scotland in Ancient Europe*, eds I. Shepherd and

G. Barclay, Society of Antiquaries of Scotland, Edinburgh, 83–90.

4. A. Shepherd and D. V. Clarke (forthcoming) *Skara Brae: A Full Compendium of the Site [from Excavations in 1972–3 and 1977 and the work of VG Childe and Earlier scholars]*, Historic Scotland, Edinburgh.

5. N. Card (2005) 'Neolithic Orkney' in *The Heart of Neolithic Orkney World Heritage Site Research Agenda*, eds J. Downes, S. Foster, C. R. Wickham-Jones and J. Callister, Historic Scotland, Edinburgh, 47–56.

6. S. Piggott (1936) 'Grooved Ware', in 'Archaeology of the submerged land surface of the Essex coast', S. H. Warren, S. Piggott, J. G. D. Clark, M. C. Burkitt, H. Godwin and M. E. Godwin, *Proceedings of the Prehistoric Society* 2, 191–201.

7. S. Piggott (1954) *The Neolithic Cultures of the British Isles*, Cambridge University Press, Cambridge.

8. T. Holden (2004) *The Blackhouses of Arnol*, Historic Scotland Research Report, Edinburgh.

9. J. Clutton-Brock (1979) 'Report on the mammalian remains other than rodents from Quanterness', in *Investigations in Orkney*, A. C. Renfrew, Society of Antiquaries of London Research Report 38, London, 112–34.

10. N. Sharples (2000) 'Antlers and Orcadian rituals: an ambiguous role for red deer in the Neolithic', in *Neolithic Orkney in its European Context*, ed. A. Ritchie, McDonald Institute Monographs, Cambridge, 107–17.

11. K. Herbert (2004) *The Explorer's Daughter*, Viking, London.

12. F. Sternke (2005) 'All are not hunters that knap the stone', in *Mesolithic Studies at the Beginning of the 21st Century*, eds N. Milner and P. C. Woodman, Oxbow Books, Oxford, 144–63.

13. G. Ehrlich (2003) *This Cold Heaven*, Fourth Estate, London.

14. C. R. Wickham-Jones (1986) 'The procurement and use of stone for flaked tools in prehistoric Scotland', *Proceedings of the Society of Antiquaries of Scotland* 116, 1–10.

15. C. R. Wickham-Jones (1977) *The flint and chert assemblage from the 1972–3 excavations at Skara Brae, Orkney*, thesis presented for the degree of MA, Department of Archaeology, University of Edinburgh, Edinburgh.

16. E. Shee Twohig (1981) *The Megalithic Art of Western Europe*, Clarendon Press, Oxford, 238–9.

17. A. Saville (1994) 'A Decorated Skaill Knife from Skara Brae, Orkney', *Proceedings of the Society of Antiquaries of Scotland* 124, 103–11.

18. A. Shepherd (2000) 'Skara Brae: expressing identity in a Neolithic Community', in *Neolithic Orkney in its European Context*, ed. A. Ritchie, MacDonald Institute Monographs, Cambridge, 139–58.

19. A. Isbister (2000) 'Burnished Haematite and Pigment Production', in *Neolithic Orkney in its European Context*, ed. A. Ritchie, MacDonald Institute Monographs, Cambridge, 191–5.

20. D. V. Clarke (1976) *The Neolithic Village at Skara Brae*, HMSO, Edinburgh.

21. A. Watson (2001) *Megalithic Sound and Landscape*, Department of Archaeology website, University of Reading, Reading (http://www.neolithic.reading.ac.uk/) (visited August 2005).

22. J. Chesterman (1983) 'The Human Skeletal Remains', in *Isbister a Chambered Tomb in Orkney*, J. W. Hedges, British Archaeological Reports 115, Oxford, 73–132.

23. J. W. Hedges (1983) 'The People of the Tombs', in *Isbister a Chambered Tomb in Orkney*, J. W. Hedges, British Archaeological Reports 115, Oxford, 273–300.

24. G. Sulzenbacher (2002) *The Glacier Mummy: Discovering the Neolithic Age with the Iceman*, Folioverlag.

25. T. Garnham (2004) *Lines on the Landscape, Circles from the Sky*, Tempus, Stroud.

26. C. Richards ed. (2005) *Dwelling Among the Monuments*, McDonald Institute Monographs, Cambridge.

Chapter Five: Maeshowe: Death, Burial and the Other World in the Late Neolithic

1. A. Challands, T. Muir and C. Richards (2005) 'The Great Passage Grave of Maeshowe', in *Dwelling Among the Monuments*, ed. C. Richards, MacDonald Institute Monographs, Cambridge, 229–48.

2. E. MacKie (1998) 'Maeshowe and the winter solstice', *Antiquity* 71, 338–59.

3. B. Ballin Smith ed. (1994) *Howe: Four Millennia of Orkney Prehistory*, Society of Antiquaries of Scotland Monograph series No. 9, Edinburgh.

4. P. J. Ashmore (1996) *Neolithic and Bronze Age Scotland*, BT Batsford and Historic Scotland, London, 60–74.

5. J. Barber (2000) 'Death in Orkney: a Rare Event', in *Neolithic Orkney in its European Context*, ed. A. Ritchie, MacDonald Institute Monographs, Cambridge, 185–7.

6. M. Dalland (1999) 'Sand Field: the excavation of an exceptional cist in Orkney', *Proceedings of the Prehistoric Society* 65, 373–413.

7. J. W. Hedges (1983) 'The Use of the Tombs', in *Isbister a Chambered Tomb in Orkney*, J. W. Hedges, British Archaeological Reports **115**, Oxford, 213–72.

8. G. J. Barclay and C. J. Russell-White (1994) 'Excavations in the ceremonial complex of the fourth to second millennium BC at Balfarg/Balbirnie, Glenrothes, Fife', *Proceedings of the Society of Antiquaries of Scotland* **123**, 43–210.

9. E. MacKie (1998) 'Maeshowe and the winter solstice', *Antiquity* **71**, 338–59.

10. N. Card (2005) 'The Neolithic World Heritage Site and Inner Buffer Zones', in *The Heart of Neolithic Orkney World Heritage Site Research Agenda*, eds J. Downes, S. Foster, C. R. Wickham-Jones and J. Callister, Historic Scotland, Edinburgh, 50–6.

11. N. Card (2003) 'Bookan Chambered Cairn', *Discovery and Excavation in Scotland 2002*, 88.

12. N. Card (2005) 'The Heart of Neolithic Orkney', *Current Archaeology* **199**, 342–7.

Chapter Six: The Brodgar Peninsula: Dances of Stones

1. S. Towrie (n.d.) 'What is a Trow', *Orkneyjar* (http://www.orkneyjar.com/folklore/trows/) (visited August 2005).

2. T. Muir (1998) *The Mermaid Bride and other Orkney folk tales*, The Orcadian, Kirkwall.

3. J. N. G. Ritchie (1985) 'Ritual Monuments', in *The Prehistory of Orkney*, ed. C. Renfrew, Edinburgh University Press, Edinburgh, 118–30.

4. C. Richards (1996) 'Skara Brae: revisiting a Neolithic village in Orkney', in *Scottish Archaeology: new perceptions*, eds W. S. Hanson and E. A. Slater, Aberdeen University Press, Aberdeen, 24–43.

5. C. Richards (2005) 'The Ceremonial House 2', in *Dwelling Among the Monuments*, ed. C. Richards, McDonald Institute Monographs, Cambridge, 129–56.

6. A. Ritchie (1995) *Prehistoric Orkney*, BT Batsford and Historic Scotland, London, 79.

7. M. Pitts (2000) *Hengeworld*, Random House, London, 190–91.

8. M. Pitts (2000) *Hengeworld*, Randon House, London, 189.

9. W. Startin (1982) 'Prehistoric earthmoving', in *Settlement Patterns in the Oxford Region*, eds H. Case and A. Whittle, Council for British Archaeology, London, 153–6.

10. M. Pitts (2000) *Hengeworld*, Randon House, London, 181–95.

11. S. Towrie (n.d.) 'Transporting the Megaliths', *Orkneyjar* (http://www.orkneyjar.com/history/brodgar/building.htm) (visited August 2005).

12. N. Card (2005) 'The Heart of Neolithic Orkney', *Current Archaeology* **199**, 342–47.

13. A. Challands, M. Edmonds and C. Richards (2005) 'Interpreting the stone monoliths', in *Dwelling Among the Monuments*, ed. C. Richards, McDonald Institute Monographs, Cambridge, 215–18.

14. A. Burl (2000) *The Stone Circles of Britain, Ireland and Brittany*, Yale University Press, New Haven.

15. T. Garnham (2004) *Lines on the Landscape, Circles from the Sky*, Tempus, Stroud,163–7.

16. A. Thom (1971) *Megalithic Lunar Observatories*, Clarendon Press, Oxford, 123.

17. C. Ruggles (1971) *Astronomy in Prehistoric Britain and Ireland*, Yale University Press, New Haven, 148.

18. S. Towrie (n.d.) 'Temples of the Sun and Moon', *Orkneyjar* (http://www.orkneyjar.com/history/brodgar/temples.htm) (visited August 2005).

19. E. Manker (1975) *People of Eight Seasons*, Nordbok, Gothenberg.

20. A. Watson and D. Keating (2000) 'The Architecture of Sound in Neolithic Orkney', in *Neolithic Orkney in its European Context*, ed. A. Ritchie, McDonald Institute Monographs, Cambridge, 259–63.

21. J. N. G. Ritchie (1976) 'The Stones of Stenness, Orkney', *Proceedings of the Society of Antiquaries of Scotland* **107**, 1–60.

22. N. Card (2005) 'The Heart of Neolithic Orkney', *Current Archaeology* **199**, 342–7.

23. A. Challands, M. Edmonds and C. Richards (2005) 'Beyond the village: Barnhouse Odin and the Stones of Stenness', in *Dwelling Among the Monuments*, ed. C. Richards, McDonald Institute Monographs, Cambridge, 205–28.

24. N. Card and S. Ovendcn (2005) 'World Heritage Area', *Discovery and Excavation in Scotland 2004*, 97.

25. R. Mabey (2005) *Fencing Paradise*, Transworld, London, 21–31.

Chapter Seven: The Wider World of the Neolithic

1. A. Henshall (1985) 'The Chambered Cairns', in *The Prehistory of Orkney*, ed. C. Renfrew, Edinburgh University Press, Edinburgh, 83–117.

2. V. G. Childe (1942) 'The Chambered Cairns of Rousay', *Antiquaries Journal* **22**, 139–42.

3. D. Fraser (1983) *Land and Society in Neolithic*

Orkney, British Archaeological Reports **117**, Oxford.

4. I. B. Barthlemess (2004) *A Celebration of Sunrise at the Tomb of the Eagles*, Orkney Museums and Heritage, Kirkwall.

5. A. Jones (1998) 'Where Eagles Dare: landscape animals and the Neolithic of Orkney', *Journal of Material Culture* **3**, 301–24.

6. V. Cummings and A. Pannett (2005) 'Island views: the settings of the chambered cairns of southern Orkney', in *Set in Stone*, eds V. Cummings and A. Pannett, Oxbow Books, Oxford, 15.

7. V. Cummings and A. Pannett (2005) 'Island views: the settings of the chambered cairns of southern Orkney', in *Set in Stone*, eds V. Cummings and A. Pannett, Oxbow Books, Oxford, 14–24.

8. N. Sharples (1985) 'Individual and community: the changing role of megaliths in the Orcadian Neolithic', *Proceedings of the Prehistoric Society* **51**, 59–77.

9. J. Barber (2000) 'Death in Orkney: a Rare Event', in *Neolithic Orkney in its European Context*, ed. A. Ritchie, McDonald Institute Monographs, Cambridge, 185–7.

10. M. Richards (2005) 'The Early Neolithic in Britain: new insights from biomolecular archaeology', in *Scotland in Ancient Europe*, eds I. Shepherd and G. Barclay, Society of Antiquaries of Scotland, Edinburgh, 83–90.

11. R. Schulting and M. Richards (2002) 'The wet, wild, and the domesticated: the Mesolithic-Neolithic transition on the West coast of Scotland', *European Journal of Archaeology* **5**, 147–89.

12. M. S. Copely, R. Berstan, S. N. Dudd, G. Docherty, A. J. Mukherjee, V. Straker, S. Payne and R. P. Evershed (2003) 'Direct chemical evidence for widespread dairying in prehistoric Britain', *Proceedings of the National Academy of Science, USA* **100**, 1524–9.

13. M. B. Richards (2003) *The Neolithic Invasion of Europe*, Yearbook of Physical Anthropology.

14. I. Hodder (1990) *The Domestication of Europe*, Blackwell, Oxford.

15. R. Mabey (2005) *Fencing Paradise*, Transworld, London.

16. R. Mabey (2005) *Fencing Paradise*, Transworld, London, 22–3.

17. R. Mabey (2005) *Fencing Paradise*, Transworld, London, 23.

18. P. J. Ashmore (1996) *Neolithic and Bronze Age Scotland*, BT Batsford and Historic Scotland, London, 73.

19. R. Butter (1999) *Kilmartin*, Kilmartin House Trust, Kilmartin.

20. J. Harding (2000) 'Later Neolithic ceremonial centres, ritual and pilgrimage: the monument complex of Thornborough, North Yorkshire', in *Neolithic Orkney in its European Context*, ed. A. Ritchie, McDonald Institute Monographs, Cambridge, 31–46.

21. J. Richards (1991) *The English Heritage Book of Stonehenge*, BT Batsford, London.

22. G. Stout (2002) *Newgrange and the Bend of the Boyne*, Cork University Press, Cork.

23. G. J. Barclay (2000) 'Between Orkney and Wessex: the search for the regional Neolithics of Britain', in *Neolithic Orkney in its European Context*, ed. A. Ritchie, McDonald Institute Monographs, Cambridge, 275–85.

Chapter Eight: The People After: The Bronze Age and the Iron Age

1. S. Øvrevik (1985) 'The Second Millennium BC and After', in *The Prehistory of Orkney*, ed. C. Renfrew, Edinburgh University Press, Edinburgh, 131–49.

2. A. Ritchie (1995) *Prehistoric Orkney*, BT Batsford and Historic Scotland, London, 86–95.

3. P. J. Ashmore (1996) *Neolithic and Bronze Age Scotland*, BT Batsford and Historic Scotland, London, 75–89.

4. N. Card (2005) 'Bronze Age Orkney', in *The Heart of Neolithic Orkney World Heritage Site Research Agenda*, eds J. Downes, S. Foster, C. R. Wickham-Jones and J. Callister, Historic Scotland, Edinburgh, 56–8.

5. D. E. Smith, A. C. De La Vega and S. Dawson (1996) 'Relative sea level changes in Orkney' in *The Quarternary of Orkney: Field Guide*, ed. A. M. Hall, Quarternary Research Association, Cambridge.

6. I. Mainland and I. A. Simpson (2005) 'Climate Change and Holocene Environments', in *The Heart of Neolithic Orkney World Heritage Site Research Agenda*, eds J. Downes, S. Foster, C. R. Wickham-Jones and J. Callister, Historic Scotland, Edinburgh, 89–92.

7. S. J. Dockrill, J. M. Bond and R. A. Nicholson (forthcoming) *Excavations at Tofts Ness, Sanday Orkney*, Society of Antiquaries of Scotland Monograph Series, Edinburgh.

8. N. Card (2005) 'The Heart of Neolithic Orkney', *Current Archaeology* **199**, 342–7.

9. J. Downes and C. Richards (2000) 'Excavating the Neolithic and Early Bronze Age of Orkney:

recognition and interpretation in the field', in *Neolithic Orkney in its European Context*, ed. A. Ritchie, McDonald Institute Monographs, Cambridge, 159–68.

10. D. A. Davidson and I. A. Simpson (1994) 'Soils and Landscape History: Case Studies from the Northern Isles of Scotland', in *The History of Soils and Field Systems*, eds S. M. Foster and T. C. Smout, Scottish Cultural Press, Aberdeen, 66–74.

11. T. G. Cowie and I. A. G. Shepherd (1997) 'The Bronze Age', in *Scotland: Environment and Archaeology, 8000 BC – AD 1000*, eds K. J. Edwards and I. B. M. Ralston, Wiley, Chichester, 151–68.

12. J. Coles and B. Coles (1995) *Enlarging the Past*, Society of Antiquaries of Scotland, Edinburgh.

13. N. Card (2005) 'Bronze Age Orkney', in *The Heart of Neolithic Orkney World Heritage Site Research Agenda*, eds J. Downes, S. Foster, C. R. Wickham-Jones and J. Callister, Historic Scotland, Edinburgh, 56–8.

14. G. Petrie (1862) 'Notice of a barrow at Huntiscarth in the parish of Harray, Orkney, recently opened', *Proceedings of the Society of Antiquaries of Scotland* 3, 201–19.

15. M. Pitts (2005) 'Orkney dig first to date gold and amber jewellery', *British Archaeology*, September/October, 7.

16. J. Downes (forthcoming) *Burial, technology and Ritual in a Landscape Setting*.

17. D. Prudames (2005) 'Divers Discover Bronze Age Wreck and Artefacts off Devon Coast', 24 Hour Museum (http://www.24hourmuseum.org.uk/nwh_gfx_en/ART 26754.html) (visited August 2005).

18. N. Card (2005) 'The Bronze Age World Heritage Site and Inner Buffer Zones', in *The Heart of Neolithic Orkney World Heritage Site Research Agenda*, eds J. Downes, S. Foster, C. R. Wickham-Jones and J. Callister, Historic Scotland, Edinburgh, 58–61.

19. I. Armit (2005) 'The Atlantic Roundhouse a beginner's guide', in *Tall Stories? Two Millennia of Brochs*, eds V. E. Turner, S. J. Dockrill, R. A. Nicholson and J. M. Bond, Lerwick, Shetland Amenity Trust, 5–10.

20. V. E. Turner, S. J. Dockrill, R. A. Nicholson and J. M. Bond (2005) *Tall Stories? Two Millennia of Brochs*, Shetland Amenity Trust, Lerwick.

21. I. Blythe (2005) 'A Military Assessment of the Defensive Capabilities of Brochs', in *Tall Stories? Two Millennia of Brochs*, eds V. E. Turner, S. J. Dockrill, R. A. Nicholson and J. M. Bond, Shetland Amenity Trust, Lerwick, 246–53.

22. J. M. Bond (2003) 'A growing success? Agricultural intensification and risk management in Late Iron Age

Orkney', in *Sea Change, Orkney and Northern Europe in the Later Iron Age, AD 300–800*, eds J. Downes and A. Ritchie, The Pinkfoot Press, Angus, 105–10.

23. H. Moore and G. Wilson (2005) 'The Langskaill Souterrain', *Current Archaeology* 199, 333–5.

24. A. Ritchie (1995) 'Earth-houses', in *Prehistoric Orkney*, ed. A. Ritchie, BT Batsford and Historic Scotland, London, 114–17.

25. J. Downes, S. Foster, C. R. Wickham-Jones and J. Callister (2005) *The Heart of Neolithic Orkney World Heritage Site Research Agenda*, Historic Scotland, Edinburgh, 145.

26. N. Dixon and B. Forbes (2005) 'Orkney Crannog Survey', in *Discovery and Excavation in Scotland 2004*, 93–4.

27. J. M. Bond (2003) 'A growing success? Agricultural intensification and risk management in Late Iron Age Orkney', in *Sea Change, Orkney and Northern Europe in the Later Iron Age, AD 300–800*, eds J. Downes and A. Ritchie, The Pinkfoot Press, Angus, 105–10.

28. I. A. Simpson (1985) *Anthropogenic Sedimentation in Orkney: the Formation of Deep Top Soils and Farm Mounds*, unpublished PhD thesis, University of Strathclyde.

29. B. Ballin Smith ed. (1994) *Howe: Four Millennia of Orkney Prehistory*. Society of Antiquaries of Scotland Monograph series No. 9, Edinburgh.

30. A. Smith (2003) 'From the small green isles to the Low Countries: artefactual evidence for contact around the North Sea basin in the later Iron Age', in *Sea Change, Orkney and Northern Europe in the Later Iron Age, AD 300–800*, eds J. Downes and A. Ritchie, The Pinkfoot Press, Angus, 111–16.

31. J. Wood (2003) 'The OrkneyOrkney Museum – an ancient recycled textile', in *Sea Change, Orkney and Northern Europe in the Later Iron Age, AD 300–800*, eds J. Downes and A. Ritchie, The Pinkfoot Press, Angus, 171–6.

32. P. J. Ashmore (2003) 'Orkney burials in the first millennium AD', in *Sea Change, Orkney and Northern Europe in the Later Iron Age, AD 300–800*, eds J. Downes and A. Ritchie, The Pinkfoot Press, Angus, 35–50.

33. H. Moore and G. Wilson (2005) 'An Iron Age 'shrine' on Westray?', *Current Archaeology* 199, 328–32.

34. N. Card, J. Downes, J. Gibson and P. Sharman (2005) 'Religion and metal working at Mine Howe, Orkney', *Current Archaeology* 199, 322–7.

35. N. Card and J. Downes (2003) 'Mine Howe – the significance of space and place in the Iron Age', in *Sea Change, Orkney and Northern Europe in the Later Iron Age, AD 300–800*, eds J. Downes and A. Ritchie, The Pinkfoot Press, Angus, 11–19.

36. A. Ritchie (1995) 'Cellars and wells', in *Prehistoric Orkney*, A. Ritchie, BT Batsford and Historic Scotland, London, 113–14.

37. M. Lück (2003) 'Traffic with the otherworld', in *Sea Change, Orkney and Northern Europe in the Later Iron Age, AD 300–800*, eds J. Downes and A. Ritchie, The Pinkfoot Press, Angus, 197–200.

38. A. Fitzpatrick (1989) 'The submission of the Orkney Isles to Claudius new evidence?', *Scottish Archaeological Review* **6**, 24–34.

Chapter Nine: Trade and Temptation: The Picts, the Norse and the Coming of Christianity

1. S. Towrie (2005) 'The Origins of Orkney', *Orkneyjar* (http://www.orkneyjar.com/placenames/orkney.htm) (visited September 2005).

2. M. Carver (1999) *Surviving in Symbols a Visit to the Pictish Nation*, Canongate and Historic Scotland, Edinburgh.

3. S. Foster (1996) *Picts, Gaels and Scots*, BT Batsford and Historic Scotland, London.

4. J. R. Hunter (1986) *Rescue Excavations on the Brough of Birsay*, Society of Antiquaries of Scotland Monograph Series no. 4, Edinburgh.

5. J. N. G. Ritchie (2003) 'Pictish Art in Orkney', in *Sea Change, Orkney and Northern Europe in the Later Iron Age, AD 300–800*, eds J. Downes and A. Ritchie, The Pinkfoot Press, Angus, 117–26.

6. D. Lawrence (2004) 'A new Pictish figure from Orkney', in *Papers and Pictures in honour of Daphne Home Lorimer MBE*, http://www.orkney-digs.org.uk/dhl/papers/dl/index.html (visited September 2005).

7. A. Ritchie (1985) 'Orkney in the Pictish Kingdom', in *The Prehistory of Orkney*, ed. C. Renfrew, Edinburgh University Press, Edinburgh, 183–209.

8. Royal Commission on the Ancient and Historical Monuments of Scotland (1994) *Pictish Symbol Stones: a Hand List*.

9. S. Foster (1996) *Picts, Gaels and Scots*, BT Batsford and Historic Scotland, London, 79–100.

10. R. G. Lamb (1995) 'Papil, Picts, and Papar', in *Northern Isles Connections, Essays from Orkney and Shetland Presented to Per Sveaas Anderson*, ed. B. Crawford, The Orkney Press, Kirkwall, 9–27.

11. A. Ritchie (1995) *Prehistoric Orkney*, BT Batsford and Historic Scotland, London, 118.

12. N. Card (2005) 'Iron Age Orkney', in *The Heart of Neolithic Orkney World Heritage Site Research Agenda*, eds J. Downes, S. Foster, C. R. Wickham-Jones and J. Callister, Historic Scotland, Edinburgh, 64.

13. A. Ritchie (1993) *Viking Scotland*, BT Batsford and Historic Scotland, London.

14. B. Smith (2003) 'Not welcome at all: Vikings and the native population in Orkney and Shetland', in *Sea Change, Orkney and Northern Europe in the Later Iron Age, AD 300–800*, eds J. Downes and A. Ritchie, The Pinkfoot Press, Angus, 145–50.

15. W. F. H. Nicholaisen (1969) 'Norse settlement in the Northern and Western Isles; some place name evidence', *Scottish Historical Review* **48**, 6–17.

16. H. J. Hjaltalin and G. Goudie trans. (1977) *The Orkneyinga Saga*, the Mercat Press, Edinburgh (facsimile of the 1873 edition published by Edmonston and Douglas).

17. C. D. Morris (1985) 'Viking Orkney: a survey', in *The Prehistory of Orkney*, ed. C. Renfrew, Edinburgh University Press, Edinburgh, 210–42.

18. S. J. Grieve and J. Gibson (2005) 'Orkney Viking Period', in *The Heart of Neolithic Orkney World Heritage Site Research Agenda*, eds J. Downes, S. Foster, C. R. Wickham-Jones and J. Callister, Historic Scotland, Edinburgh, 66–9.

19. S. J. Grieve and J. Gibson (2005) 'Orkney Late Norse Period', in *The Heart of Neolithic Orkney World Heritage Site Research Agenda*, eds J. Downes, S. Foster, C. R. Wickham-Jones and J. Callister, Historic Scotland, Edinburgh, 69–71.

20. A. Ritchie (1993) *Viking Scotland*, BT Batsford and Historic Scotland, London, 33–5.

21. S. J. Hunter, J. M. Bond and A. N. Smith eds (forthcoming) *Investigations at Pool, Sanday, Orkney*, Society of Antiquaries of Scotland Monograph Series, Edinburgh.

22. S. Buteux (1997) *Settlements at Skaill, Deerness, Orkney – excavations by Peter Gelling*, British Archaeological Report 260, Oxford.

23. C. D. Morris (1993) 'The Birsay Bay Project, a resume', in *The Viking Age in Caithness, Orkney, and the North Atlantic*, eds C. E. Batey, J. Jesch and C. D. Morris, Edinburgh University Press, Edinburgh, 285–307.

24. A. Ritchie (1977) 'Excavation of Pictish and Viking Farmsteads at Buckquoy, Orkney', *Proceedings of the Society of Antiquaries of Scotland* **108**, 174–227.

25. J. Barrett (2005) 'Farming and Fishing on Medieval Westray', *Current Archaeology* **199**, 336–41.

26. S. J. Grieve and J. Gibson (2005) 'Orkney Late Norse Period', in *The Heart of Neolithic Orkney World Heritage Site Research Agenda*, eds J. Downes, S. Foster, C. R. Wickham-Jones and J. Callister, Historic Scotland, Edinburgh, 69–71.

27. R. MacLeod (1994) *Building St Magnus Cathedral, Kirkwall*, HALMAC publishing, Shetland.

28. L. Burgher (1991) *Orkney, an Illustrated Architectural Guide*, Royal Incorporation of Architects in Scotland, Edinburgh.

29. R. G. Lamb (1993) 'Congress Diary', in *The Viking Age in Caithness, Orkney, and the North Atlantic*, eds C. E. Batey, J. Jesch and C. D. Morris, Edinburgh University Press, Edinburgh, 44–9.

30. B. Crawford (1987) *Scandinavian Scotland*, Leicester University Press, Leicester.

31. P. J. Ashmore (2003) 'Orkney burials in the first millennium AD', in *Sea Change, Orkney and Northern Europe in the Later Iron Age, AD 300–800*, eds J. Downes and A. Ritchie, The Pinkfoot Press, Angus, 35–50.

32. O. Owen and M. Dalland (1999) *Scar, a Viking Boat Burial on Sanday, Orkney*, Tuckwell Press, Edinburgh.

33. M. P. Barnes (1994) *The Runic Inscriptions of Orkney*, Uppsala University, Uppsala.

34. A. Challands M. Edmonds and C. Richards (2005) 'Barnhouse Odin', in *Dwelling Among the Monuments*, ed. C. Richards, McDonald Institute Monographs, Cambridge, 207–11.

35. S. Towrie (n.d.) 'The Odin Stone and the Orcadian Wedding', *Orkneyjar*, (http://www.orkneyjar.com /history/odinstone/odwedd.htm) (visited September 2005)

36. W. P. L. Thomson (2001) *A New History of Orkney*, Birlinn, Edinburgh.

37. S. J. Grieve and J. Gibson (2005) 'Orkney Viking Period', in *The Heart of Neolithic Orkney World Heritage Site Research Agenda*, eds J. Downes, S. Foster, C. R. Wickham-Jones and J. Callister, Historic Scotland, Edinburgh, 66–69.

38. J. Graham-Campbell and C. E. Batey (1998) *Vikings in Scotland: an Archaeological Survey*, Edinburgh University Press, Edinburgh.

39. D. Griffiths (2005) 'Bay of Skaill', *Discovery and Excavation in Scotland 2004*, 95.

Chapter Ten: Farmland, Famine and Visitors: Historic Orkney into the Twentieth Century

1. B. E. Crawford (2003) 'Orkney in the Middle Ages', in *The Orkney Book*, ed. D. Omand, Birlinn Ltd, Edinburgh, 64–81.

2. F. Wainwright (1962) *The Northern Isles*, Nelson, London, 190–1.

3. G. Donaldson (1990) *A Northern Commonwealth*, The Saltire Society, Edinburgh.

4. S. J. Grieve and J. Gibson (2005) 'Late medieval Orkney', in *The Heart of Neolithic Orkney World Heritage Site Research Agenda*, eds J. Downes, S. Foster, C. R. Wickham-Jones and J. Callister, Historic Scotland, Edinburgh 71–4.

5. W. P. L. Thomson (2001) *A New History of Orkney*, Birlinn, Edinburgh, 233–46.

6. P. Andersen (2003) 'The Reformation and the Stewart Earls', in *The Orkney Book*, ed. D. Omand, Birlinn Ltd, Edinburgh, 81–92.

7. P. D. Anderson (1982) *Robert Stewart Earl of Orkney, Lord of Shetland*, John Donald, Edinburgh.

8. Attributed to J. Emerson (1652) *Poetical descriptions of Orkney*.

9. M. P. Barnes (1998) *The Norn Language of Orkney and Shetland*, Shetland Times, Lerwick.

10. W. P. L. Thomson (1986) 'Pict, Norse, Celt and Lowland Scot', in *The People of Orkney*, eds R. J. Berry and H. N. Firth, Orkney Press, Kirkwall, 209–24.

11. S. J. Grieve and J. Gibson (2005) 'Late medieval Orkney', in *The Heart of Neolithic Orkney World Heritage Site Research Agenda*, eds J. Downes, S. Foster, C. R. Wickham-Jones and J. Callister, Historic Scotland, Edinburgh, 71–4.

12. W. P. L. Thomson (2001) *A New History of Orkney*, Birlinn Ltd, Edinburgh.

13. W. P. L. Thomson (2003) 'Agricultural Improvement', in *The Orkney Book*, ed. D. Omand, Birlinn Ltd, Edinburgh, 93–101.

14. W. P. L. Thomson (1983) *Kelp-making in Orkney*, The Orkney Press, Kirkwall.

15. S. J. Grieve and J. Gibson (2005) 'Post medieval Orkney', in *The Heart of Neolithic Orkney World Heritage Site Research Agenda*, eds J. Downes, S. Foster, C. R. Wickham-Jones and J. Callister, Historic Scotland, Edinburgh, 74–7.

16. R. P. Fereday (1986) 'The Lairds and Eighteenth Century Orkney', in *The People of Orkney*, eds R. J. Berry and H. N. Firth, Orkney Press, Kirkwall, 225–45.

17. J. Coull (2003) 'Fishing', in *The Orkney Book*, ed. D. Omand, Birlinn Ltd, Edinburgh, 144–55.

18. S. Towrie (n.d.) 'The Hudson's Bay Company', *Orkneyjar* (http://www.orkneyjar.com/orkney/ stromness/hbs.htm) (visited September 2005).

19. J. Wallace (1700) *An Account of the Islands of Orkney*, Jacob Tonson, London.

20. J. Gourlay (2003) 'Tourism', in *The Orkney Book*, ed. D. Omand, Birlinn Ltd, Edinburgh, 156–66.

21. S. Wenham (2003) 'Modern Times', in *The Orkney Book*, ed. D. Omand, Birlinn Ltd, Edinburgh, 102–14.

22. Fleet Air Arm Archive, *HMS Furious* (http://www.fleetairarmarchive.net/Ships/FURIOUS.h tml) (visited September 2005).

23. S. Wenham (2003) 'Modern Times' in *The Orkney Book*, ed. D. Omand, Birlinn, Edinburgh, 102–14.

24. S. Wenham (2003) 'Modern Times' in *The Orkney Book*, ed. D. Omand, Birlinn, Edinburgh, 102–14.

25. H. Blair (n.d.) *The Orkney Blast*.

26. S. Callaghan (2003) 'St Magnus Cathedral, Kirkwall', in *The Orkney Book*, ed. D. Omand, Birlinn Ltd, Edinburgh, 167–74.

27. T. Muir (2003) 'Customs and Traditions', in *The Orkney Book*, ed. D. Omand, Birlinn Ltd, Edinburgh, 269–74.

28. P. Leith (1937) 'The Bellendens and the Palace of Stenness', *Proceedings of the Orkney Antiquarian Society* **14**, 41–4.

29. P. Leith (1937) 'The Bellendens and the Palace of Stenness', *Proceedings of the Orkney Antiquarian Society* **14**, 41–4.

30. J. N. G. Ritchie (1976) 'The Stones of Stenness, Orkney', *Proceedings of the Society of Antiquaries of Scotland* **107**, 1–60.

31. J. Ben (1529) 'Inscripto Insularum Orchadiarum', in *Geographical Collections relating to Scotland made by Walter MacFarlane, vol. 3*, A. Mitchell and J. T. Clark (1908) Scottish Historical Society no. 53, Edinburgh.

32. J. Farrer (1862) *Notice of Runic Inscriptions Discovered During Recent Excavations in the Orkneys*, Edinburgh.

33. I. Sandison (2000) *Orkney Visitor Survey 2000 Report Summary*. (http://www.scotexchange.net /orkney_2000_summary.pdf) (visited September 2005).

Chapter Eleven: Antiquarians and Archaeologists

1. B. G. Trigger (1989) *A History of Archaeological Thought*, Cambridge University Press, Cambridge, 263.

2. G. Barry (1805) *History of the Orkney Islands*, Constable, Edinburgh.

3. J. Wallace (1693) *A Description of the Islands of Orkney*, Jacob Tonson, Edinburgh.

4. F. W. L. Thomas (1852) 'An account of some of the Celtic antiquities of Orkney, including the Stones of Stenness, tumuli, Picts houses etc with plans', *Archaeologia* **34**, 88–136.

5. F. E. Ellesmere (1848) *Guide to Northern Archaeology*, James Bain, London.

6. G. Petrie (1867) 'Notice of ruins of ancient dwellings at Skara, Bay of Skaill in the parish of Sandwick, Orkney, recently excavated', *Proceedings of the Society of Antiquaries of Scotland* **7**, 201–19.

7. C. Darwin (1859) *The Origin of Species*, Harvard University Press, Cambridge, Mass. (and http://www.literature.org/authors/darwin-charles/the-origin-of-species/index.html) (visited September 2005).

8. W. Traill (1885) 'Notice of Excavations at Stenabreck and Howmae in N Ronaldsay, Orkney', *Proceedings of the Society of Antiquaries of Scotland* **19**, 14–33.

9. W. Turner (1903) 'An Account of a Chambered Cairn and Cremation Cists at Taversoe Tuick, near Trumland House, in the Island of Rousay, Orkney, excavated by Lieut. General Traill Burroughs, C.B., of Rousay, in 1898', *Proceedings of the Society of Antiquaries of Scotland* **37**, 73–82.

10. R. S. Clouston (1885) 'Notice of the excavation of a chambered cairn of the Stone Age, at Unstan, in the Loch of Stennis, Orkney', *Proceedings of the Society of Antiquaries of Scotland* **19**, 341–5.

11. http://ads.ahds.ac.uk/catalogue/ARCHway/volume Selector.cfm?rcn=1340 (visited September 2005)

12. RCAHMS (1946) *Twelfth Report with an Inventory of the Ancient Monuments of Orkney and Shetland*, HMSO, Edinburgh.

13. D. Wilson (1851) *Archaeology and Prehistoric Annals of Scotland*, Macmillan, Edinburgh.

14. H. Marwick (1929) 'Skerrabrae', *Proceedings of the Orkney Antiquarian Society* **7**, 37–40.

15. S. Piggott (1936) 'Grooved Ware', in S. H. Warren, S. Piggott, J. G. D. Clark, M. C. Burkitt, H. Godwin and M. E. Godwin, 'Archaeology of the submerged land surface of the Essex coast', *Proceedings of the Prehistoric Society* **2**, 191–201.

16. J. G. Callander (1931) 'Notes on (1) certain prehistoric relics from Orkney and (2) Skara Brae, its culture and period', *Proceedings of the Society of Antiquaries of Scotland* **65**, 78–114.

17. V. G. Childe and W. G. Grant (1947) 'A Stone Age settlement at the Braes of Rinyo, Rousay, Orkney', *Proceedings of the Society of Antiquaries of Scotland* **81**, 16–42.

18. S. Green (1981) *Prehistorian, a Biography of Vere Gordon Childe*, Moonraker Press, Bradford-on-Avon.

19. G. Daniel (1981) *A Short History of Archaeology*, Thames and Hudson, London.

20. B. G. Trigger (1980) *Gordon Childe, Revolutions in Archaeology*, Thames and Hudson, London.

21. W. Traill and W. Kirkness (1937) 'Howar, a prehistoric structure on Papa Westray', *Proceedings of the Society of Antiquaries of Scotland* **71**, 309–21.

22. V. G. Childe (1956) 'Maes Howe', *Proceedings of the Society of Antiquaries of Scotland* **88**, 155–72.

23. V. G. Childe (1952) 'Re-excavation of the chambered cairn of Quoyness, Sanday, on behalf of the Ministry

of Works in 1951–2', *Proceedings of the Society of Antiquaries of Scotland* **86**, 121–39.

24. A. S. Henshall (1963) *The Chambered Tombs of Scotland*, Edinburgh University Press, Edinburgh.

25. B. G. Trigger (1989) *A History of Archaeological Thought*, Cambridge University Press, Cambridge.

26. A. C. Renfrew (1973) *Before Civilisation: that Radiocarbon Revolution and Prehistoric Europe*, Cape, London.

27. I. Hodder (1982) *Symbolic and Structural Archaeology*, Cambridge University Press, Cambridge.

28. A. C. Renfrew (1979) *Investigations in Orkney*, Society of Antiquaries Research Report no. 38, London.

29. D. V. Clarke (1976) 'Excavations at Skara Brae, a summary account', in *Settlement and Economy in the Third and Second Millennium BC*, eds C. Burgess and R. Miket, British Archaeological Reports no. 33, Oxford, 233–47.

30. A. Ritchie (1983) 'Excavation of a Neolithic Farmstead at Knap of Howar, Papa Westray, Orkney', *Proceedings of the Society of Antiquaries of Scotland* **113**, 40–121.

31. J. N. G. Ritchie (1976) 'The Stones of Stenness, Orkney', *Proceedings of the Society of Antiquaries of Scotland* **107**, 1–60.

32. J. R. Hunter (1986) *Rescue Excavations on the Brough of Birsay*, Society of Antiquaries of Scotland Monograph Series no. 4, Edinburgh.

33. C. D. Morriss (1976) 'Brough of Deerness, Orkney, Excavations 1975: Interim Report', *Northern Studies* **7–8**, 33–7.

34. J. W. Hedges (1975) 'Excavation of two Orcadian burnt mounds at Liddle and Beaquoy', *Proceedings of the Society of Antiquaries of Scotland* **106**, 39–99.

35. D. A. Davidson and R. L. Jones (1985) 'The Environment of Orkney', in *The Prehistory of Orkney*, ed. C. Renfrew, Edinburgh University Press, Edinburgh, 10–35.

36. D. V. Clarke and N. Sharples (1985) 'Settlements and subsistence in the third millennium BC', in *The Prehistory of Orkney*, ed. C. Renfrew, Edinburgh University Press, Edinburgh, 54–82.

37. J. Barber (1997) *The Excavation of a Stalled Cairn at the Point of Cott, Westray, Orkney*, STAR monograph series no. 1, Edinburgh.

38. O. Owen (1984) *The Archaeological Rescue Project at Tuquoy, Westray, Orkney*, Universities of Durham and Newcastle upon Tyne Archaeological Report no. 7.

39. N. Sharples (1984) 'Excavations at Pierowall Quarry, Westray, Orkney', *Proceedings of the Society of Antiquaries of Scotland* **114**, 75–126.

40. S. Dockrill (1986) 'Resistivity survey of two settlement sites at Tofts Ness, Sanday, Orkney', *Proceedings of the Society of Antiquaries of Scotland* **116**, 561–5.

41. C. Richards ed. (2005) *Dwelling Among the Monuments*, McDonald Institute Monographs, Cambridge.

42. A. Ritchie ed. (2000) *Neolithic Orkney in its European Context*, McDonald Institute Monographs, Cambridge.

43. J. Downes and A. Ritchie eds (2003) *Sea Change, Orkney and Northern Europe in the Later Iron Age, AD 300–800*, The Pinkfoot Press, Angus.

44. http://www.orkney.uhi.ac.uk/html/archaeology/archaeology.htm (visited September 2005).

45. N. Card, J. Downes, J. Gibson and P. Sharman (2005) 'Religion and metal working at Mine Howe, Orkney', *Current Archaeology* **199**, 322–7.

46. H. Moore and G. Wilson (2005) 'An Iron Age 'shrine' on Westray?', *Current Archaeology* **199**, 328–32.

47. N. Card (2005) 'The Heart of Neolithic Orkney', *Current Archaeology* **199**, 342–7.

48. http://www.orkneycommunities.co.uk/FOAT/ (visited September 2005)

49. http://www.orkney.gov.uk/nqcontent.cfm?a_id=443 (visited September 2005)

50. http://www.orcadian.co.uk/ (visited September 2005); http://www.orkneytoday.ltd.uk/index.asp (visited September 2005)

51. http://www.orkneycommunities.co.uk/radio OrkneySchedule.asp (visited September 2005)

52. http://whc.unesco.org/ (visited September 2005)

Chapter Twelve: World Heritage Status: The Ultimate Accolade?

1. A. McClanahan (2004) *The Heart of Neolithic Orkney in its Contemporary Contexts*, Historic Scotland, Edinburgh. Downloadable from http://www.historic-scotland.gov.uk/index/publications/worldhsites publications (visited September 2005).

2. D. Miles (2005) *The Tribes of Britain*, Weidenfeld and Nicolson, London.

3. B. Bender (1998) *Stonehenge: Making Space*, Berg, London.

4. L. V. Prott (1992) 'A common heritage: the World Heritage Convention', in *All Natural Things*, eds L. Macinnes and C. R. Wickham-Jones, Oxbow Books, Oxford, 65–86.

5. http://whc.unesco.org/ (visited September 2005).

6. P. Fowler (2004) *Landscapes for the World*, Windgather Press Ltd, Macclesfield.

7. http://whc.unesco.org/en/conventiontext/ (visited September 2005).

8. Historic Scotland (1998) *Nomination of the Heart of Neolithic Orkney for Inclusion in the World Heritage List*, Historic Scotland, Edinburgh.

9. http://whc.unesco.org/en/comittee/ (visited September 2005).

10. http://www.icomos.org/ICOMOS_Main_Page.html (visited September 2005).

11. http://www.international.icomos.org/e_introd.htm #membership (visited September 2005).

12. National Trust for Scotland, *St Kilda*, http://www.kilda.org.uk/ (visited September 2005).

13. *Edinburgh World Heritage*, http://www.ewht.org.uk/ (visited September 2005).

14. *New Lanark*, http://www.newlanark.org/ (visited September 2005).

15. Historic Scotland, *Statement of Significance*, http://www.historic-scotland.gov.uk/index/policy andguidance/world_heritage_scotland/world_heritage_ sites/world-heritage-neolithic-orkney.htm (visited September 2005).

16. Historic Scotland (1998) *Nomination of the Heart of Neolithic Orkney for Inclusion in the World Heritage List*, 5.

17. Historic Scotland (1998) *Nomination of the Heart of Neolithic Orkney for Inclusion in the World Heritage List*, 5.

18. Historic Scotland (1998) *Nomination of the Heart of Neolithic Orkney for Inclusion in the World Heritage List*, 5.

19. Historic Scotland (1998) *Nomination of the Heart of Neolithic Orkney for Inclusion in the World Heritage List*, 5.

20. Historic Scotland (1998) *Nomination of the Heart of Neolithic Orkney for Inclusion in the World Heritage List*, 5–9.

21. English Heritage, *What Are World Heritage Sites?* http://www.english-heritage.org.uk/server /show/conWebDoc.4194 (visited September 2005).

22. Historic Scotland (2001) *The Heart of Neolithic Orkney Management Plan*, http://www.historic-scotland.gov.uk/index/publications/worldhsites publications/whsorkneypublications.htm #orkney_management_ plan (visited September 2005).

23. S. M. Foster and L. Linge (2002) 'World Heritage Site buffer zones. Statements of fact or aspiration?', *Conservation and Management of Archaeological Sites* 5, 141–50.

24. http://www.historic-scotland.gov.uk/index/publica-tions/worldhsitespublications/whsorkneypublications (visited September 2005).

25. J. Downes, S. Foster, C. R. Wickham-Jones and J. Callister eds (2005) *The Heart of Neolithic Orkney World Heritage Site Research Agenda*, Historic Scotland, Edinburgh, fig. 10, 27.

26. V. Cummings and A. Pannett eds (2005) *Set in Stone*, Oxbow Books, Oxford.

27. P. Fowler (2004) *Landscapes for the World*, Windgather Press, Macclesfield, 94–5.

28. N. Card (2005) 'The Heart of Neolithic Orkney', *Current Archaeology* **199**, 342–7.

29. J. Downes and S. M. Foster (2005) 'Management of the WHS', in *The Heart of Neolithic Orkney World Heritage Site Research Agenda*, eds J. Downes, S. Foster, C. R. Wickham-Jones and J. Callister, Historic Scotland, Edinburgh, 25–35.

30. G. Barry (1805) *History of the Orkney Islands*, Constable, Edinburgh.

31. UNESCO, *Convention for the Protection of Cultural Property in the Event of Armed Conflict*, http://www.unesco.org/culture/laws/hague/ html_eng/page1.shtml (visited September 2005).

As this book went to press three new volumes appreared and all are a good read (and useful):

Muir, T. (2006) *The Shorter Orkneyinga Saga*, Orkney Museums and Heritage, Kirkwall

Muir, T. ed. (2006) *Orkney in the Sagas*, Orkney Museums and Heritage, Kirkwall

Owen, O. ed. (2006) *The World of Orkneyinga Saga*, Orkney Museums and Heritage, Kirkwall

Index

....

numbers in bold/italics denote pages where illustrations appear